THE CLOSEST THING
IN HISTORY

The Fab Four
and the
Younger Romantics

THE CLOSEST THING IN HISTORY

The Fab Four
and the
Younger Romantics

John Webster

John Webster Publications
Oxford

First published in Great Britain in 2024
by John Webster Publications
© John Webster 2024

Every effort has been made to use and reference quotations within
fair use conventions. In the event of any queries please contact the
author at webstjohn@gmail.com

ISBN 978-1-0683328-0-7

Front cover graphics:

The Beatles arriving at JFK airport, 1964.
Public Domain, adapted by Andy Severn.
Younger Romantics illustration
© John Webster Publications.

Acknowledgements

With thanks to the work of Barnette Miller whose 1910 book on Leigh Hunt was foundational, a salutation to the memory of Brian Thompson for his gift of Anthony Holden's biography of Hunt, thanks also to Anthony and Anne Swift for friendship and encouragement, to Nora Crook for Romantics-related chinwaggery, to Barbara Hudson for casting a creative eye over a draft front cover, to Dave Eastoe for alerting me to Jenny Boyd's 'It's Not Only Rock 'n' Roll', to Bonnier Books for permission to quote from it, to Robin Stewart for the back cover photograph, to Premila and Jonathan for support and suggestions, to Benjamin Zephaniah for his love of 'the gang', to my sister Alison for making a huge contribution at the proofreading stage, to the good-hearted Romantics scholars who have corresponded with me outside their circle of responsibilities, and to Ruth Murray for her disinterested assistance.

I should also explain that the *Quarterly Review*, which played such an oppositional role in the story of the Romantics, has quietly helped out by contributing the break symbol below and on the pages dividing each section.

This book is dedicated
to the memory of
Benjamin Zephaniah

When people ask me

'Where does
your inspiration
come from?'

I always say:

'If I knew *that* ...
... I would go there'.

Contents

Introduction

The Beatles' first press agent Tony Barrow finished his memoir by saying: 'The Beatles hadn't happened before, and would never happen again'. At the time of their split it may have seemed that such groups were natural to pop culture, but today, more than fifty years later, it seems that he was right.

However, he may not have been totally correct in saying that they 'hadn't happened before'. Because, if one thinks outside of the box and goes back to the early decades of the 19th century, another cluster of creative talents of the same order and influence as The Beatles *can* be found: the poets known as the Younger Romantics – John Keats, Lord Byron, Leigh Hunt and Percy Bysshe Shelley.

They certainly lived through parallel times. Barnette Miller's description of the Romantics' era as a time when people 'were clamouring for freedom from the trammels of the past and were pressing forward to the new day' could just as well be a description of the 1960s. As could Shelley's description of his own time, as one in which creative spirits were both leading and accompanying some great subterranean shift in consciousness and political change:

'The great writers of our own age … are the companions and forerunners of some unimagined change in our social condition or the opinions which cement it. The cloud of mind is discharging its collected lightning'.

i

What follows invites the reader to cast off the apparent distinctions between classic poetry and rock 'n' roll, bring the eras of the Romantics and The Beatles together, and engage with both, toggling between them in a playful yet fertile exercise.

It could well be objected such a comparison seems 'a bit of a stretch'. After all, they worked in different media, and had very different trajectories of fame. Most of all, The Beatles were a creative unity while the individual poets worked separately, with Keats and Byron never even meeting. So the first chapters will lay out some broad parallels between the two groups which will hopefully allay such doubts. The middle section will tell the story of the Younger Romantics through a Beatles-like lens, focussing mainly on their interactions but also giving a sense of their poetic development and bringing in Beatles-related insights where they occur.

The scene will then be set for some intriguing perspectives to appear. As Mark Twain put it, 'History never repeats itself, but it does often rhyme'. As we can trace the Romantics' legacy, it should be possible, if the comparison has been accepted, to make some educated guesses at how The Beatles will continue to influence our era. An understanding of how the Romantics prepared the ground for The Beatles may emerge, together with a sense that inspiration, hard work, care, talent and vision can yield real and measurable results in human history. We can even guess at when 'the next Beatles' might arise and what such a new phenomenon could look like.

Noel Coward will appear in these pages in a not entirely flattering light, miffed that the new force of The Beatles had emphatically superseded his own songwriting achievements. Compared to Beatles songs his own seem much wordier, and to go back further in time to the era of the Romantics is to enter a world where the word was even more central. So to bring the 19th and 20th century worlds together is to present something of a two-speed reading experience, with the latter slipping easily into the mind and the former requiring more focus. I hope to have achieved the right balance between the two.

Growing up with The Beatles and feeling bereft when they split up, I found another source of inspiration in the Romantic poets in the mid-1970s, which eased that sense of loss. The process of getting to know them involved encounters with a wonderful array of scholars and writers, not only knowledgeable about their particular poet but also about their social and political environment. It will be a great pleasure to me if this book can introduce some of these scholars whose fascinating and canny work I am hugely indebted to.

I am also indebted to contemporary internet bloggers and Beatles websites for providing information and insights: an intensive immersion in episodes from Chris Shaw's 'I am the Eggpod' podcast in particular let me into a huge range of perspectives on The Beatles. It was particularly fascinating to hear the different processes by which new generations had encountered them, giving an insight into The Beatles' staying power and enduring appeal. And when the cultural historian John Higgs said that The Beatles were a 'transcendent, culture-shifting' force he put his finger on the key quality that unites the two groups and distinguishes them from other musicians and poets.

The mass media world we now inhabit can be seen as an exploded diagram of the world of the Romantics, with The Beatles an exploded version of the earlier poets. Much has changed, but should the overall assumption behind this book, an intuition that rock 'n' roll has become a vehicle for popular poetic insights become clear, we will be left with the knowledge that Keats's words, 'The poetry of earth is never dead', still ring true.

– John Webster 2024

PART ONE

Parallels

1 From Tintern Abbey
to Heartbreak Hotel

William Wordsworth and Elvis Presley might well seem to be an unlikely pairing. However, both were vital influences on the groups who built on their respective legacies: the Younger Romantics in the early 19th century and The Beatles in the mid-20th. In addition, both ended up disappointing and then turning on their protégés.

In May 1956 Elvis Presley entered the British charts with 'Heartbreak Hotel', and soon after, the 16 year-old John Lennon, listening to his radio in his bedroom at night, first heard the sound that would energise and propel his career. It emerged out of apparent nothingness and was so unlike the well-groomed, well-enunciated singers of before, with Elvis's vocal hiccupping and echoing against its bluesy background. Thirty years later, at a ceremony inducting Elvis into the Rock 'n' Roll Hall of Fame, Julian Lennon read a direct quote from his father: 'Elvis was the thing, whatever people say, he was it. I was not competing against Elvis, rock happened to be the media I was born into - it was the one, that's all. Those people who picked up paintbrushes, like Van Gogh, probably wanted to be Renoir or whomever went before him. I wanted to be Elvis'.

George Harrison also talked of the overwhelming impact of 'Heartbreak Hotel'. For him too it was like nothing he had ever heard and seemed to be like a sound pulling towards the future, away from the post-war depression Britain was still struggling with. In fact, he said later, it was 'like the sound of hope'.

For Ringo, Elvis was a herald of a new and youthful power, using rock 'n' roll to express teenage realities; for Paul he was hot, he was an idol; he hammed things up and did 'funny little things' that somehow broke with day to day realities. And as a singer he was a true great: not only did his phrasing and his use of echo on 'Heartbreak Hotel' mesmerise the young Paul, it even sounded as if he was singing 'from the depths of Hell'. For all four then, Elvis provided the inspiration that would fire them up and show them the path they could travel. John Lennon summed it up: 'without Elvis there would have been no Beatles'.

Could one say that Wordsworth had a similar impact on the Younger Romantics? The answer is yes, with qualifications. His 'Lyrical Ballads', published in 1798, contained the key poem 'Tintern Abbey', and the second edition included a preface that would prove as influential in its time as Elvis was a century and a half later.

Wordsworth's attraction to the younger poets rested primarily on his identification of Nature as a spiritual resource. 'Tintern Abbey' had the crucial passage:

For I have learned
To look on nature, not as in the hour
Of thoughtless youth; but hearing oftentimes
The still, sad music of humanity,
Nor harsh nor grating, though of ample power
To chasten and subdue. And I have felt
A presence that disturbs me with the joy
Of elevated thoughts; a sense sublime
Of something far more deeply interfused,

2

Whose dwelling is the light of setting suns,
And the round ocean and the living air,
And the blue sky, and in the mind of man;
A motion and a spirit, that impels
All thinking things, all objects of all thought,
And rolls through all things. Therefore am I still
A lover of the meadows and the woods,
And mountains; and of all that we behold
From this green earth; of all the mighty world
Of eye, and ear, — both what they half create,
And what perceive; well pleased to recognise
In nature and the language of the sense,
The anchor of my purest thoughts, the nurse,
The guide, the guardian of my heart, and soul
Of all my moral being.

Just as Elvis in his early career brought radically new directions to popular music, so Wordsworth departed from the classical values that drove the 'Augustan era' poetry of the 18th century – the emphasis on 'order, logic, balance, propriety, reason and mastery of the emotions'.

Augustan poetry may well have given the English language classic and enduring lines, like Alexander Pope's pithy, shrewd expressions: 'To err, is human; to forgive divine'; 'Fools rush in where angels fear to tread'; 'A little knowledge is a dangerous thing' and 'Hope springs eternal in the human breast'. However, in his Preface to the 1802 edition of 'Lyrical Ballads' Wordsworth had put the expression of feeling, rather than of neatly conveyed maxims, at the centre of his artistic project: 'I have said that

Poetry is the spontaneous overflow of powerful feelings: it takes its origin from emotion recollected in tranquillity…' What is more, he linked poetry with pleasure: 'the mind will upon the whole be in a state of enjoyment'.

Wordsworth could be as harsh about the poets of the 18th century as rock 'n' rollers could be about the generally manufactured songs of the pre-rock 'n' roll years: he called Samuel Johnson's poem 'The Ant' 'a dreadful hubbub of words'. The shared criticism was that the work was emotionally bogus and artistically dull.

In Shelley's case his friend Thomas Love Peacock would recall that 'Shelley devotedly admired Wordsworth'; he ordered the 1800 edition of 'Lyrical Ballads' in 1812, and after returning from his elopement with Mary Godwin (and being desperately short of money) acquired, for two guineas – Wordworth's 'The Excursion' – described by William St Clair as 'perhaps the most expensive work of literature ever published in England'. Wordsworth's phrases found their way into his work, with the 'harsh and grating' expression from 'Tintern Abbey' surfacing in 'The Revolt of Islam':

> One echo of a world of woes
> The harsh and grating strife of tyrants and of foes.

As for Keats, the influence of Wordsworth was well set out by the writer Colin Silver, who showed that the introspective and meditative quality of Wordsworth's 'Prefatory Sonnet' – neither 'harking after an irretrievable past nor dreaming about a possibly non-existent future' – transferred itself into Keats's first published poem, 'To Solitude'.

Wordsworth had written:

> Nuns fret not at their Convent's narrow room;
> And Hermits are contented with their Cells;
> And Students with their pensive Citadels:
> Maids at the Wheel, the Weaver at his Loom,
> Sit blithe and happy; Bees that soar for bloom,
> High as the highest Peak of Furness Fells,
> Will murmur by the hour in Foxglove bells:
> In truth, the prison, unto which we doom
> Ourselves, no prison is: and hence to me,
> In sundry moods, 'twas pastime to be bound
> Within the Sonnet's scanty plot of ground:
> Pleas'd if some Souls (for such there needs must be)
> Who have felt the weight of too much liberty,
> Should find short solace there, as I have found.

Keats, living alone in grimy lodgings in London, adopted its tone and looked for a similar sense of high purpose behind his isolation:

> O Solitude! If I must with thee dwell,
> Let it not be among the jumbled heap
> Of murky buildings: climb with me the steep, -
> Nature's observatory – whence the dell,
> In flowery slopes, its river's crystal swell,
> May seem a span; let me thy vigils keep
> 'Mongst boughs pavilioned, where the deer's swift leap
> Startles the wild bee from the foxglove bell.
> But though I'll gladly trace these scenes with thee,

> Yet the sweet converse of an innocent mind,
> Whose words are images of thoughts refined,
> Is my soul's pleasure; and it sure must be
> Almost the highest bliss of human-kind,
> When to thy haunts two kindred spirits flee.

Like Wordsworth's poem, it argues for a type of fulfilment that can be found in solitude – for Wordsworth in the craft of poetry, but also, for Keats, in nature and in friendship: 'Almost the highest bliss of human-kind'. Thanks to Leigh Hunt, who printed it in *The Examiner* in May 1816, 'To Solitude' became his first published poem and was an important step on his poetic journey. So it is not an exaggeration to say that Wordsworth opened the door for Keats.

Leigh Hunt himself was an admirer of Wordsworth: he had both published and reviewed his work in *The Examiner*, and described him as the 'prince of bards'. In 1817 he gave Wordsworth a generous accolade: 'But it is Mr. Wordsworth who has advanced it [poetry] the most, and who in spite of some morbidities as well as mistaken theories in other respects, has opened upon us a fund of thinking and imagination, that ranks him as the successor of the true and abundant poets of the older time'.

He even 'had the honour of a visit from Mr. Wordsworth. He came to thank me for the zeal I had shewn in advocating the cause of his genius. I had the pleasure of shewing him his book on my shelves by the side of Milton; a sight which must have been the more agreeable, inasmuch as the visit was unexpected'.

Byron was the exception, with a distinctly conflicted attitude to the older poet. Devoted to Pope as he was, and with his own work stylistically rooted in the classical poetry of the 18th century, Wordsworth did not have this critical influence on his development. Yet when he reviewed Wordsworth's 1807 collection his tone was measured. On the one hand he acknowledges that the earlier 'Lyrical Ballads' has 'not undeservedly met with a considerable share of public applause', and that 'many of the poems' in the 1807 publication 'possess a native elegance, natural and unaffected' but argues that 'When Mr W. ceases to please' it is because he expresses 'the most common place ideas … in language that is not simple but puerile'. 'On the whole, however' (with some exceptions) 'these volumes display a genius worthy of higher pursuits….'

When, a few years later, he lambasted the literary establishment in 'English Bards and Scotch Reviewers', a poem once described as 'the nastiest poem in the English language', he included Wordsworth in his attack:

> Next comes the dull disciple of thy school,
> That mild apostate from poetic rule,
> The simple WORDSWORTH, …
> … Who, both by precept and example, shows
> That prose is verse, and verse is merely prose;
> Convincing all, by demonstration plain,
> Poetic souls delight in prose insane;
> And Christmas stories tortured into rhyme
> Contain the essence of the true sublime.

His conclusion was: 'Let simple WORDSWORTH chime his childish verse'…

Surprisingly though, when he met Wordsworth some years later – he wrote that he 'had but one feeling from the beginning of the visit to the end – reverence'. And a year later, in Switzerland, he got closer to Wordsworth's pantheistic worldview thanks to Shelley: 'Shelley, when I was in Switzerland, used to dose me with Wordsworth physic even to nausea; and I do remember then reading some things of his with pleasure'.

So the younger poets, with the qualified exception of Byron, found inspiration in Wordsworth.

Meeting one's hero in person though, can be notoriously disconcerting, as The Beatles found when they dropped in on Elvis at his Los Angeles home in 1965. Though cordial, the atmosphere was edgy, with Tony Barrow recalling that Elvis was 'uncomfortably self-conscious'. It was the height of Beatlemania, and Elvis must have felt threatened by the new force The Beatles represented. However, as his most recent release had topped the charts in the US and the UK, he had felt secure enough to meet them. For Ringo, one major issue was his entourage, who he found sycophantic. Another problem was his apparent fall from rock 'n' roll grace, with his glory days behind him. This also bothered John Lennon, who asked him why sentimental ballads had replaced the inspirational rock that had so inspired him. 'What happened to good old rock 'n' roll?' Tony Barrow remembered him asking.

Characteristically Lennon had got to the heart of the problem for each individual Beatle. George Harrison, who attended one of his concerts in Madison Square Gardens in 1972, described his decline as 'sad'. Though 'he did a couple of good tunes' his big band could not hide, for George, his loss of his original spirit. And his Vegas period fatally punctured Paul's previous admiration for him, leading him to lose interest in his former idol completely.

So there was all-round disenchantment amongst The Beatles about their erstwhile hero's artistic direction, with general agreement with John Lennon's comment that he 'died when he went in the army. That's when they killed him. The rest of it was just a living death'.

Very similar was the Younger Romantics own disillusion with Wordsworth. In his youth he had hymned the French Revolution in his famous words from 'The Prelude': 'Bliss was it in that dawn to be alive/But to be young was very heaven'.

Now he had abandoned his youthful radicalism and had accepted a government post as Distributor of Stamps for Westmoreland. It paid £400 per annum and gave him financial security, but, of course, aligned him with the ruling elite who were opposing the political reforms the Younger Romantics yearned for.

Keats first encountered Wordsworth in December 1817, when he was in full establishment mode, and had a slightly off-putting experience, as his friend the painter Benjamin Haydon recalled:

'When Wordsworth came to Town I brought Keats to him, by his Wordsworth's desire – Wordsworth received him kindly, & after a few minutes, Wordsworth asked him what he had been lately doing, I said he has just finished an exquisite Ode to Pan – and as he had not a copy I begged Keats to repeat it – which he did in his usual half chant, (most touching) walking up & down the room – when he had done I felt really, as if I had heard a young Apollo – Wordsworth drily said

'a Very pretty piece of Paganism' –
This was unfeeling, & unworthy of his high Genius to a young Worshipper like Keats -- & Keats felt it deeply'.

Yet this encounter did not lead to a complete break; Keats was always fair-minded towards Wordsworth and acknowledged his poetic gifts, maintaining that 'Tintern Abbey' had shown 'he is a Genius and superior to us ....' and even that 'Wordsworth is deeper than Milton'. His meetings with Wordsworth, however, had shown him another side of the poet. 'I am sorry that Wordsworth has left a bad impression wherever he visited in Town— by his egotism, Vanity and bigotry— yet he is a great Poet' he had written to his brothers in February.

There was 'a Wordsworth he admired and a Wordsworth for whom he felt a profound distaste', and a few years later he would have a reminder of Wordsworth's politics when he visited the Lake District to find that the elder poet was supporting the Tory candidate Lord Lowther and his brother Henry against the reformer (and friend of Leigh Hunt) Henry Brougham.

The election also registered with Shelley, who responded to Thomas Love Peacock after he had told him of Brougham's defeat, and Wordsworth's contributions to the campaign. According to Peacock, Wordsworth had written their pamphlet 'Two Addresses to the Freeholders of

Westmoreland', and had argued that 'they ought not to choose so poor a man as Brougham, riches being the only guarantees of political integrity'.

'What a beastly and pitiful wretch that Wordsworth!' wrote Shelley. 'That such a man should be such a poet! I can only compare him with no one but Simonides, that flatterer of Sicilian tyrants and at the same time the most natural and tender of lyric poets'.

Shelley was seriously troubled by what he saw as Wordsworth's defection, and kept returning to the subject. In his sonnet 'To Wordsworth', he focused on his own sense of loss now that Wordsworth has abandoned his youthful radicalism and his devotion, when he was 'as a lone star', to 'truth and liberty'.

> Poet of Nature, thou hast wept to know
> That things depart which never may return:
> Childhood and youth, friendship and love's first glow,
> Have fled like sweet dreams, leaving thee to mourn.
> These common woes I feel. One loss is mine
> Which thou too feel'st, yet I alone deplore.
> Thou wert as a lone star, whose light did shine
> On some frail bark in winter's midnight roar:
> Thou hast like to a rock-built refuge stood
> Above the blind and battling multitude:
> In honoured poverty thy voice did weave
> Songs consecrate to truth and liberty,—
> Deserting these, thou leavest me to grieve,
> Thus having been, that thou shouldst cease to be.

Wordsworth's defection continued to haunt him: in 'An Exhortation' he makes 'a kind of excuse for Wordsworth', suggesting that the reason that the poet 'changed (his) hue' was a 'lack of love'. But in the third of his poems about Wordsworth he abandoned his playful and forgiving tone. Following the publication of Wordsworth's narrative poem 'Peter Bell' in 1819, which was instantly parodied by Keats's friend John Hamilton Reynolds, he weighed in with the comic satire 'Peter Bell the Third', themed themed around Wordsworth's political volte-face and artistic decline. Though the sell-out Wordsworthian poet of 'Peter Bell' was able to achieve a Graceland-style abode:

> He hired a house, bought plate, and made
> A genteel drive up to his door,
> And sifted gravel neatly laid,
> As if defying all who said,
> Peter was ever poor…

he was nevertheless, as The Beatles all saw the post-army Elvis, an example of a 'living death'.

> But a disease soon struck into
> The very life and soul of Peter…

For though

> He walked about—slept—had the hue
> Of health upon his cheeks…
> And yet a strange and horrid curse
> Clung upon Peter, night and day;
>
> Peter was dull—he was at first
> Dull—oh, so dull—so very dull!
> Whether he talked, wrote, or rehearsed
> Still with this dullness was he cursed—

Dull, beyond all conception—dull.

Powering this attack was not only Shelley's disappointment at Wordsworth's political apostasy. He also saw the older poet as betraying poetry itself, not only abandoning the vital nature-based vision of his early work but turning his back on Shelley's own conception of poetry as an activist social force. This was a real and bitter division between the two poets, for Wordsworth saw the pantheistic, nature-centred creed of 'Tintern Abbey' as merely a stepping stone to greater truths contained in Christian doctrine, while for Shelley such attitudes were more all-embracing.

Later on there would be an unmistakeable falling out between the older poet and his younger rivals. For when news broke that Shelley, Byron and Leigh Hunt were coming together in Pisa to launch a journal, Wordsworth was horrified, writing:

'Byron, Shelley and Leigh Hunt are to lay their heads together in some town in Italy for the purpose of conducting a journal to be directed against everything in religion, morals, and probably in government and literature which our forefathers have been accustomed to reverence'.

Thus the Younger Romantics' father figure turned on his younger acolytes, paralleling the deteriorating relationship between Elvis and The Beatles. For almost exactly 150 years later, Elvis Presley, meeting with President Nixon in the White House in 1970, launched 'into a passionate diatribe against the Beatles. He claimed: 'The Beatles came to this country, made their money, and then returned to England where they promoted an anti-American theme'. At which Ringo said 'That's very sad to me that he felt so threatened, and that he felt like a lot of people, that we were bad for the

13

American youth'. As for Paul, he reckoned that 'He ended up a complete plonker, unfortunately—he turned in the end, wanted to become a Federal drug marshal'.

By and large then, The Beatles and the Younger Romantics both had their inspirational 'father figure' who helped to set them on their creative roads but disappointed them in the end, both artistically and by their betrayal of their early ideals. Yet there remained a residue of affection: Jerome McGann argues that lines in Byron's satire 'The Vision of Judgement', where St Michael addresses Satan (on the point of leaving the ranks of angels to begin his Satanic career), can be seen as summarising, in a regretful but still respectful tone, his approach to Wordsworth:

> Our different parties make us fight so shy,
> I ne'er mistake you for a *personal* foe;
> Our difference is *political,* and I
> Trust that, whatever may occur below,
> You know my great respect for you; and this
> Makes me regret whate'er you do amiss.

An anticipation of George Harrison's comment on Elvis? 'But we all loved Elvis and it was sad to see what happened to him. We still love him and he's still there in his spirit and in his music and best of luck to him. That's what I say'.

2
Inspiration from Plato to Pop

Right at the end of his life, in the last interviews he gave, John Lennon returned over and over again to his experience of the mysterious quality of inspiration that could be regarded as the fundamental driving force behind his work and that of the other Beatles. To Dave Sholin and Laurie Kaye he said that though he could, if necessary, write a song to order he never enjoyed that, preferring the songs that came out of nowhere. An example of that, he told *Playboy Magazine*, were the lyrics of 'Across the Universe', which were entirely inspirational and came out of nowhere.

His first wife Cynthia had had something on her mind, and was venting her concerns. But instead of writing a grouchy response he came up with a beautifully tangential lyric drawn from his recent experience of transcendental meditation. Feeling irritable, he had got out of bed, gone downstairs, and put it down on paper, not even wanting to write it. Only then could he get some sleep. It was as if the song wasn't connected with him: he didn't own it and it was in an extraordinary and unrepeatable metre. There was craftsmanship writing, but this was something else, which was more like being possessed, a state which had been behind his earlier songs 'Nowhere Man' and 'In My Life'.

The connection between The Beatles and the Younger Romantics is clear, with his accounts echoing Shelley's attempt to describe the mysterious quality of inspiration. 'The mind in creation' he wrote in 'A Defence of Poetry', 'is as a fading coal, which some invisible influence, like an inconstant wind, awakens to transitory brightness'.

Anyone who has been on a tour of The Beatles' homes in Liverpool will appreciate that they were hardly born with silver spoons in their mouths. John Lennon's home on Menlove Avenue is the most salubrious, but his original home at 9 Newcastle Rd, was an ordinary terraced house; two of George Harrison's early homes were modest 'two up and two downs', Paul McCartney's later home a becoming modern council house, and Ringo's homes in Madryn St and Admiral Grove in the Dingle area of Liverpool the most basic of them all.

All a long way from the more upscale childhoods of the Younger Romantics. The poshest of the lot was Lord Byron. Though he had been brought up in financial straits due to his father's raids on his mother's fortune, at school in Aberdeen, at the age of ten, the young Byron was called into the headmaster's study, given cakes and wine, patted on the head, and told that he had now become a Lord. Four years earlier, thanks to the death of his grandfather's son in battle, Byron had become the heir presumptive to the title. Now, with grandpa's death, though still lacking financial security, he had a new home – the monumental pile of Newstead Abbey near Nottingham.

Shelley was the son of a baronet, with his family home being the impressive Field Place near Horsham (where each stone roof tile weighed two tons). Keats – though far from an aristocrat with his father (before his death when Keats was 9) running a thriving stables in Moorgate in London – could fall back on family money while trying to earn his keep as a poet. Leigh Hunt, though so famously impecunious that he was later caricatured as Skimpole in Charles Dickens' Bleak House', was, like the others, well educated at a private school.

Despite these differences in birth and education, and the differences between Pop music and Romantic poetry, both groups were united by their occupation of the same imaginative landscape. Shelley's 'A Defence of Poetry' was highly influenced by Plato's Socratic dialogue 'Ion; or, of the Iliad' which he'd translated sometime between 1819 and 1821. It's fascinating to note that Lennon's last interviews, with his descriptions of the creative process – 'It's like being *possessed,* like a psychic or a medium' – were effectively echoing Plato.

'Ion' begins with Socrates meeting up with the lyric poet of the same name, who is returning to Athens after winning first prize for poetry at Epidaurus. Ion has a query: how is that he excels at reciting and interpreting Homer, but 'with respect to other poets I am deserted of this power'. He asks Socrates to 'consider what may be the cause of this distinction'.

Socrates begins by saying '*you* are not the master of any art … but it is a divine influence that moves you, like that in the stone called Magnet by Euripides… For not only does this stone possess the power of attracting iron rings, but it can communicate to them the power of attracting other rings. … And as the power of the stone circulates through all the rings of this series, and attaches each to each, so the

Muse, communicating through those whom she has first inspired, to all others capable of sharing in the inspiration, the influence of that first enthusiasm, creates a chain and a succession. For the authors of those great poems which we admire, do not attain to excellence through the rules of any art, but they utter their beautiful melodies of verse in a state of inspiration, and, as it were, possessed by a spirit not their own'.

Socrates concludes that a poet cannot 'compose anything worth calling poetry until he becomes inspired, and, as it were, mad, or whilst any reason remains in him'. His or her work 'is excellent in proportion to the extent of his participation in the divine influence, and the degree in which the Muse itself has descended on him …. Does it seem to you that I am in the right, O Ion?'

'Yes, by Jupiter!' says Ion; 'My mind is enlightened by your words, O Socrates…'

All this was key to Shelley's conception of poetry and its origins as set out in 'A Defence of Poetry'. Shelley's view was that inspiration could not be summoned up at will, it was a gift, and that in the 'intervals of inspiration', as he put it, 'the poet becomes mortal again' So the rock 'n' roller who began life in a terraced house at 9 Newcastle Road in Liverpool is perfectly in accord with the son of a baronet born in Field Place near Horsham, one Percy Bysshe Shelley.

What about Shelley's fellow poets? In Pisa, with Shelley and Byron in close proximity and Shelley enjoying his company, but also feeling outclassed by Byron in terms of the success of his work, he was quoted by Trelawny as saying that 'If Byron were inspired with Socrates' divine madness he would eclipse what he has yet done; his faculties are dimmed by the pernicious platitudes of his London visitors'.

But Byron would laugh off Shelley's earnestness: 'Gin and water is the source of all my inspiration' is a line in one of his letters which one can imagine him teasing Shelley with, and you only have to look at his satire 'The Vision of Judgement', which draws energy from the worlds of contemporary gossip, politics and entertainment to see that actually, the more Byron was immersed in the social world the more vibrant and pertinent his work became.

In fact, Byron can be interpreted as playing endless roles in his work. Not only does he, as in 'Childe Harold', tease the reader with characters based to some (but what?) degree on himself, but overall his approach is 'playful, cynical, perverse', using techniques of masking, ventriloquism and undercutting to complicate the reader's understanding of his work.

For example, his famous lines on Greek freedom in 'Don Juan' (which we know, as he gave his life for the cause, came from his heart) were voiced by a transparently insincere songster, a turncoat and a 'sad trimmer'. So Byron complicates any straightforwardly patriotic or ennobling feelings the reader might feel by introducing a cynical perspective. He does the same thing in his poem 'Mazeppa' which tells of the Ukrainian patriot of the same name: Mazeppa finishes his stirring tale to find his main listener, the king of Sweden – fast asleep!

As Jerome McGann puts it, 'Byron's writing begins and thrives in disillusion' – his 'lyric style is romanticism's dark angel' – and contemporary reviewers often took him to task for his flippancy and irony. One reviewer wrote: 'The mischief that lurks in all Lord Byron's productions is this – they are lying representations of human nature; they bring qualities of a most contradictory kind into close alliance; and so shape them into seeming union to confound sentiments…, which … should for ever be kept contrasted, and at polar extremities with respect to each other'.

Despite Shelley's admiration for Byron's poetry, his flippancy was a constant challenge to the Shelley who believed in the redeeming force of poetry, and that 'hope is a solemn duty we owe alike to ourselves and to the world'. To have Byron as a daily companion in Pisa was not easy; as Trelawny put it: 'Byron's wit and humour might force a grim smile, or hollow laugh … but they savoured more of pain than playfulness, and made you dissatisfied with yourself and him. When I left his gloomy hall, and the echoes of the heavy iron-plated door died away, I could hardly refrain from shouting with joy as I hurried along the broad-flagged terrace which overhangs the pleasant river… to the hospitable and cheerful abode of the Shelleys. There I found those sympathies and sentiments which the Pilgrim [Byron] denounced as illusions believed in as the only realities….'

Nevertheless Byron did subscribe to a conception of writing that stresses the original impulse; as he wrote to his publisher John Murray (who was getting increasingly anxious about the tone and content of 'Don Juan') 'With regard to what you say of retouching Don Juan, it is all very well; but I can't furbish. I am like the tiger (in poesy), if I miss my first Spring, I go growling back to my Jungle. There is no second. I can't correct; I can't, and I won't. … You must take my things as they happen to be … I don't say that you are not right: I merely assert that I cannot better them. And there's an end'.

As for Keats, there are various accounts of his approach to his work. His friend Richard Woodhouse recalled: 'He has repeatedly said in conversation that he never sits down to write, unless he is full of ideas—and then thoughts come about him in troops as though soliciting to be accepted and he selects—one of his Maxims is that if Poetry does not come naturally it had better not come at all'.

'He has said that he has often not been aware of the beauty of some thought or expression until after he had composed and written it down.—It has then struck him with astonishment, and seemed rather the production of another person than his own.—He has wondered how he came to hit upon it. This was the case with the description of Apollo in the 3rd book of Hyperion It seemed to come by chance or magic—to be as it were something given to him'. How very similar to Paul McCartney's description of how 'Yesterday' was written. He had woken up with this wonderful tune running round his head, found the chords to it on his piano, thought 'that's a nice tune', but because it came from a dream couldn't believe he had written it.

Plato's Socrates had theorised about the creative process, giving it a semi-religious twist; another theory, attributed to the French novelist Alphonse Daudet, could be added in at this point. He was described as believing 'that in the case of all creators there are accumulations of sentient force made without their knowledge. Their nerves, in a state of high excitation, register visions, colours, forms, and odours in those half-realised reservoirs which are the treasuries of poets. All of a sudden, through some influence or emotion, through some accident of thought, these impressions meet with the suddenness of a chemical reaction'. That description of mental reservoirs, freed by some inner compulsion into a song, poem, or other work of art, could well be seen as describing how Beatles songs like 'Across The Universe', 'Here Comes The Sun' and 'Hey Jude' as well as poems from the Romantics like the 'Ode to the West Wind', 'To Autumn' or 'The Prophecy of Dante' came into being.

It was surely this unconscious tapping into the zone of inspiration that made The Beatles' work such a surprising and pioneering companion. Elvis Costello would recall that having grown up with Beatles songs he was totally thrown when 'Revolver' was released. 'The music was so strange and yet so vivid' he said later, adding that the album then became an indispensable part of his life.

An experience felt by so many across the world, where The Beatles were fulfilling Shelley's conception of poetry as a force that 'lifts the veil from the hidden beauty of the world, and makes familiar objects be as if they were not familiar'. As we shall see, the Younger Romantics would inspire and influence each other in different ways but The Beatles, working in the new format of the rock band, would bring this mutual inspiration closer. They would make it work in a shared and interacting format rather than as a solitary dynamic, a powerful development and one of the gifts they have bequeathed to humanity. There is the solitary poet of tradition and there is the contemporary band of today, pioneered by The Beatles – ('the Ur-band', as Alice Cooper once described them) – and creating songs with lyrics powered by a running current of music. 'So that's how you do it' said Tom Petty when he first saw them in the USA.

Even after the band had disbanded they were still influencing each other. 'F*** a pig, it's Paul!' said John Lennon when Paul's 'Coming Up' came on the radio as he was being driven round Cold Harbor Springs on Long Island in early 1980. 'I thought 'Coming Up' was great' he said later, and it sparked off the train of creativity that led to 'Double Fantasy' and 'Milk and Honey' – 'Suddenly I got the songs'.

3

Byronic fame and Beatlemania

Jenny Boyd, the sister of George Harrison's wife Patti, once remembered George telling her that 'he found The Beatles' huge influence on society quite baffling'.

'I thought it was pretty strange why we made the enormous impact that we did – or have still. It's strange how the chemistry between the four of us made this big thing that went right through the world. There wasn't any country in the world, even the most obscure places, that didn't know about The Beatles – from grandparents to babies. It just blanketed everything, and that amazed me more than anything. We always felt that if we could get the right record contract, we'd be successful. But our tiny little concept of success that we had at the time was nothing compared to what happened. It was just enormous. It does make one think there's more to this than meets the eye.'

Ringo Starr was also surprised with the public reaction, saying that he was just trying to play the best that he could and not really focusing on the wider implications of what was happening.

Yet the scale of events could not be ignored. Remembering The Beatles' concert at Shea Stadium forty years on, Paul, (whose youthful ambition was that one day he might be able to work as a cabaret singer) noted its awesome and groundbreaking nature. It was their biggest show yet, and, in addition, the first ever stadium concert.

Playing to 56,000 people was like being in 'some mad dream' he said, 'It was thrilling, terrifying…' Beatlemania was like being at the eye of the hurricane, and George's sense of something mysterious at its heart was shared by John Lennon: 'This isn't just showbusiness' he once said.

Although the scale of Beatlemania was unprecedented, Lord Byron was also catapulted into a world of fame, as exhilarating, puzzling, frightening and ego-boosting as that of The Beatles 150 years later.

His epic narrative poem 'Childe Harold's Pilgrimage' was an instant hit: 'I awoke and found himself famous' Byron wrote after its publication in 1812. The actual sales of his work may be dwarfed by today's pop hits but in that era, with a much smaller audience, they were still sensational. The first deluxe edition 'sold its complete run of 500 copies at 30 shillings a copy within three days of its publication on 10 March 1812. A second octavo edition at 12 shillings followed shortly afterwards, reaching a tenth edition in 1814, after which the first two cantos were incorporated into joint publications with cantos III and IV, or in larger collected editions'.

Just like a modern pin up there was sex appeal in the mix as well: he remembered later that 'the number of anonymous portraits and letters I received, and all from English ladies, would be enough to fill a large volume'. 'That pale face is my fate' Lady Caroline Lamb said to herself when she saw Byron across a crowded room. Young women poured their hearts out to him: 'I very much fear that his head begins to be turned by all the adoration of the world, especially the women' wrote one lady who met Byron in May 1812.

Influenced by the phenomenon young men, including Keats, adopted a Byronic persona, just as Beatles fans would later adopt Liverpool accents. The Duchess of Devonshire wrote to a friend in the aftermath of 'Childe Harold': 'The subject of conversation, of curiosity, of enthusiasm almost, one might say, is not of Spain or Portugal, Warriors or Patriots, but Lord Byron'.

Though the enticing combination of sex appeal and an exciting new addition to contemporary culture underlay Beatle- and Byron-manias, there was something deeper happening. Unwittingly Byron and The Beatles had tapped into an unseen popular need, and though there was obvious delight in achieving fame and popularity there was also a frightening aspect of being at being at the centre of a popular storm.

An essay by the Romantics scholar Richard Cronin, 'Mapping Childe Harold I and II', analyses the deeper reasons for the impact of Byron's poem, and can be seen as addressing George Harrison's comment: 'It does make one think there's more to this than meets the eye.' 'Childe Harold's Pilgrimage', with its 9-line Spencerian stanza format, may lack immediacy in our 21st century, multimedia, digitized environment but at the time it was electrifying. It was often read aloud, which gave it a rhythmic dynamic that fuelled its popular appeal.

The story begins with a young man of dissolute habits, 'a youth', who 'spent his days in riot most uncouth'.

Eventually, bored with his depraved lifestyle and 'With pleasure drugged', 'in joyless reverie', 'he almost longed for woe', 'And from his native land resolved to go'. Soon he is in Portugal, where in Lisbon harbour 'a thousand keels did ride/Of mighty strength, since Albion was allied, and to the Lusians [Portuguese] did her aid afford'.

In short, the Byron/Childe Harold character had landed in the very seat of the long-running war with revolutionary and then Napoleonic France, the event that in one form or another had occupied the national mind in Britain for two decades.

In response to the war, Cronin argues, the poetry of the era 'seemed condemned to be either loud or tinkling, either to promulgate shrilly the patriotic fervour of a nation at war or retreat into a lyric voice fit only for the expression of private sentiment'.

One of these poems was John Wilson Croker's 1810 poem 'The Battles of Talavera', which celebrated Wellington's victories there. Then, spurred on by Walter Scott's complaint about 'the apparent apathy of our poets and rhymers to the events passing over them' the following years produced a series of poems about the war 'in which individual sentiment is subordinated to the communal and introspection is absorbed into patriotism'.

Another, 'A vision of Don Roderick', was by Scott himself, and Cronin notes the anachronistic motivation behind the work, a desire to transfer the 'warrior virtues of a feudal society to the early nineteenth century'. Byron, he explains, makes fun of the anachronism by using archaic language in one of the opening stanzas, also noting that

Harold is a 'degenerate representative of the chivalric tradition':

> Childe Harold was he hight:—but whence his name
>   And lineage long, it suits me not to say;
> Suffice it, that perchance they were of fame,
>   And had been glorious in another day:
>   But one sad losel soils a name for aye,
>   However mighty in the olden time…

Cronin argues that Byron's device of choosing a hero who is so 'alienated from his family, his friends and his nation serves a wider function: it allows the whole poem to bear witness to a fact of modern experience that it is in Scott's interest to deny, the fact of self-consciousness, the existence of a self that cannot be subsumed within any larger affiliation to a group or to a nation'. He concludes: 'It was the stance that Byron had developed in response to war', his 'subordination of public sentiment to individual feeling', that proved so fascinating to his readers.

In other words a society that was mentally tied to the events of the Napoleonic wars was suddenly presented with a character who was traversing the war-scapes that had been occupying their imaginations, but was refusing to let them overawe him. Unlike the 'loud or tinkling' poems that stemmed from an uncomplicated patriotic response, 'Childe Harold' suddenly set people's inner lives free. The fact that its hero was a complex, contradictory, capricious figure, with his own feelings rather than 'public sentiment' at centre stage, acted to release people's sense of themselves; Byron, for the rest of his life, would be an object of interest and regard because of this service he had unwittingly performed.

'Childe Harold' had something else in its favour which enabled it to sidestep censure from the government-supporting Tory literary journals of the day. Though the liberal bias of the young author was obvious, that did not alienate Tory reviewers, because, as Cronin says, though 'Childe Harold' 'was unmistakably a Whig poem' it 'recognises bitterly that Whig principles cannot be coherently applied to the Europe through which Byron conducts his reader'. Staunch Tories could hardly object, and though this recognition of impotence seems 'an unpromising accomplishment … it was the achievement that secured the poem's extraordinary success.'

It was a trick The Beatles also pulled off, as shown by a canny piece of sequencing on the first album to be released in America by Capitol Records, 'Meet the Beatles!' 'For some people in the States their presence was seen as really subversive, somehow dangerous, somehow scary' said Christine Feldmann-Barrett, author of 'A Women's History of the Beatles'. For the Philadelphia-published *Catholic Standard and Times* the Beatles were 'wholly unsuitable for children': not only was rock 'n' roll regarded by some as a 'degraded' form of music, but, as Feldmann-Barrett notes, 'there was the reaction of girls out in the streets, surrounding the Plaza Hotel, screaming and crying and just being taken over by the moment … the whole young female reaction … was something that scared … this is not the way young ladies behave in public – what the hell is going on?'

Though the album opened with 'I want to hold your hand', with its orgasmic-sounding vocal line 'I can't hide, I can't hide, I can't HIDE' and continued with the pure rocker 'I saw her standing there', the next track 'This Boy' acted as a reassurance. As Feldmann-Barrett put it: 'You have these two out and out rockers ... and then you go into this very gentle, thoughtful sounding ballad with that ... doowop sensibility baked into it. I really could see a teenage girl's Mom walking into her bedroom while she's listening to that ... and the Mom asking her daughter – 'Who's this?' And when she finds out it's The Beatles, she's genuinely shocked'.... She didn't think they were capable of producing those kinds of songs'.

So in both Byron's and the Beatles' rise to fame there was a convergence of factors that all worked together. Their success affected their peers in similar ways, from the 'spontaneous envy' which can be the greatest compliment a fellow artist can pay to another, through to the sour and patronising response of an older, now overshadowed great.

In the Beatles' case, Mick Jagger revealed in 1988 that 'Love Me Do' had almost overwhelmed him with envy. Not only did The Beatles have a record contract, but they had this record in the charts, and with a bluesy harmonica too. It was a combination, he confessed, that made him feel 'almost sick.'

He also talked later about how The Beatles had affected the Rolling Stones, explaining that Keith Richards had driven him crazy by immersing himself in Beatles music, realizing that they had to move from being a blues band to a pop band, and they had to learn to write songs like the Beatles were producing. 'We [were] undeniably the blues band, but we knew we had to be a pop band.'

Bob Dylan was hugely impressed by the fact that the Beatles, in April 1964, occupied the top five positions of the *Billboard* Hot 100 chart. 'It was wild' he said. Their electric rock sound was also an important factor in moving him away from folk music, and, he told *Rolling Stone* magazine in 1969, he envied the Beatles their easy access to the best musical back up: 'Anything they want to put on their record, they just call up and it's there. I'd like to be in that position'.

Noel Coward represented the sour and patronising response. The Beatles, he maintained, were 'little boys who should be seen and not heard' and, though 'the two I met, seemed nice, pleasant young men' they were, of course, 'totally devoid of talent'. As for the fans, he described them as 'squealing young maniacs' and would have liked to have 'cracked their heads together'. Unsurprisingly, when he went to visit the Beatles later Brian Epstein told him they hadn't been very pleased by his comments in the press and didn't want to say hello.

However, there was a postscript. Coward asked Epstein's assistant to go get one of the Beatles, and McCartney came out. 'I explained gently but firmly that one did NOT pay much attention to the statements of newspaper reporters... The poor boy was quite amiable and I sent messages of congratulations to his colleagues'. However, Coward said that despite these remarks to McCartney, he considered them 'bad-mannered'.

A century and a half earlier his response was prefigured by Wordsworth's, who felt unjustly overshadowed by the glamorous new poet of the day. Two months after 'Childe Harold' had been published he wrote to his wife Mary: 'Yesterday I dined alone with Lady B.—and we read Lord Byron's new poem which is not destitute of merit; though ill-planned, and often unpleasing in the sentiments, and almost always perplexed in the construction'.

As for Walter Scott, he would recognise that he had been comprehensively superseded, precisely as Noel Coward would be later by The Beatles, and Cronin finishes his article by noting that the publication of 'Childe Harold' led to Scott's decision to abandon poetry for the novel – 'there would have been little wisdom in measuring my forces against so formidable an antagonist'.

Shelley, near the end of his life, with the famous Byron close at hand and reminding him of his own failure to reach an audience, wrote to a friend reflecting on 'Childe Harold' and Byron's rise to fame: 'Lord Byron is in this respect fortunate. He touched a chord to which a million hearts responded, and the coarse music he produced to please them disciplined him to the perfection he now approaches'.

Which, incidentally, if you disregard the word 'coarse', could be a description of The Beatles' own artistic progression, from their joyous Moptop days to their reinvention of pop music itself.

PART TWO

The 'First Fab Four' 1813-1824

4
Come Together ... over Leigh

If the Younger Romantics are seen as 19th century forerunners of the Beatles, then the question arises – which of the poets corresponds to which of the Fab Four? Clearly the personalities cannot match exactly, but the creative dynamic of Lennon and McCartney may be seen as corresponding to that of Byron and Shelley, while George Harrison's artistic journey can be compared to that of Keats, long overshadowed but delivering, at the end, some of the group's finest work. Perhaps the best match comes with the least well known of the four, Leigh Hunt, who can be seen as occupying the same position as Ringo in the group.

As Granpa said to Ringo in 'A Hard Days's Night': 'Where would they be without your steady backbeat?' Paul McCartney is on record as agreeing with his fictional grandad, remembering how Ringo's drumming first kicked in behind them one evening in Hamburg:

'One night, our drummer then, Pete Best, wasn't available, so Ringo sat in. I remember the moment. Pete was great and we had a great time with him, but me, John, and George — God bless 'em — were on the front line singing, which we usually were, and behind us, we had this guy we'd never played with before. And I remember the moment when he started playing, I think it was Ray Charles' 'What'd

I Say,' and most of the drummers couldn't nail the drum part. It was a little difficult to do, but Ringo nailed it. Ringo nailed it.

'And I remember the moment, just standing there and looking at John and then looking at George, and the look on our faces was all like 'F***. What is this?' And that was the moment. That was the beginning, really, of the Beatles'.

In a similar way Leigh Hunt's contribution would support, anchor and power the work of Keats, Shelley and Byron. Like Ringo he was the eldest, and just as Ringo, as John Lennon put it, 'was a star in his own right in Liverpool before we even met', he was a major literary and journalistic personality of the day. Leigh Hunt had established himself as an influential critic and editor before the writing careers of Byron, Shelley and Keats had begun. He made his name firstly as a youthful poetic prodigy, and developed into a witty and outspoken theatre critic. He next branched into political comment after launching the liberal newspaper *The Examiner* with his brother John in 1807. Campaigning vigorously for Parliamentary reform and the abolition of the slave trade, opposing the death penalty and abuses in the military, *The Examiner* also included a strong literary strand. This combination of poetry and politics made him an influential and sympathetic figure in the worlds of the younger poets.

However, just as no one has ever seriously maintained that Ringo had songwriting skills to match his bandmates, so Hunt could never match up to Keats, Shelley or Byron in creative terms. Nevertheless, both still did pretty well, with two of Ringo's songs, 'Don't Pass Me By' and 'Octopus's Garden' making it onto the 'White Album' and 'Abbey Road' respectively. In his solo career a succession of songs charted in the American Top Ten including 'It Don't Come Easy', 'Back off Boogaloo', and 'Photograph', while his cover version of 'You're Sixteen' went all the way to No 1.

Like Ringo, Leigh Hunt also did well in the USA, as borne out by a charming story he told in his autobiography about his 'Story of Rimini', published in 1816:

'The Story of Rimini' had not long appeared when I received a copy of it, which looked like witchcraft. It was the identical poem in type and appearance, bound in calf, and sent to me without any explanation; but it was a little smaller. I turned it over a dozen times, wondering what it could be, and how it could have originated. The simple solution of the puzzle I did not consider, till I had summoned other persons to partake my astonishment. At length we consulted the title page, and there saw the names of 'Wells and Lilly, Boston; and M. Carey, Philadelphia'. – I thought how the sight would have pleased my mother and father…'

Also, just like Ringo, he made some telling creative contributions to the group's work. He has two poems in Palgrave's Golden Treasury, 'Rondeau', better known as 'Jenny Kissed Me', and 'Abou ben Adhem' with its timeless humanistic message. His autobiography would be a lasting testimonial to the poets he befriended and championed.

When, provoked by the lavish and sycophantic celebrations for the Prince Regent's 40th birthday, he described Prince Regent in *The Examiner* as a 'fat Adonis of 40', he and his brother John were both charged with libel. The judge ruled that the article was indeed a 'scandalous and defamatory libel', aimed at attacking 'a person who was to be looked upon as filling the first situation in the government of the country' and imposed a two year jail sentence on the brothers, also fining each £500.00.

In effect, Hunt was responsible for the first coming together of the group, for Keats, Byron and Shelley were each, separately, outraged by the sentence, and the young poets all, in their different ways, rallied round him. Byron visited him in his prison cell in Southwark jail (which he had famously filled with books and decorated as a flower garden). He would defer to the older man, despite his own burgeoning career and reputation, even informing him that his youthful poems had inspired him to become a poet. Shelley pledged £20.00 in support, and Keats wrote one of his better early poems, a 'protest sonnet', you could say, on his release:

Written on the Day that Mr Leigh Hunt Left Prison

What though, for showing truth to flattered state,
Kind Hunt was shut in prison, yet has he,
In his immortal spirit, been as free
As the sky-searching lark, and as elate.
Minion of grandeur! think you he did wait?
Think you he nought but prison-walls did see,
Till, so unwilling, thou unturnedst the key?
Ah, no! far happier, nobler was his fate!

In Spenser's halls he strayed, and bowers fair,
Culling enchanted flowers; and he flew
With daring Milton through the fields of air:
To regions of his own his genius true
Took happy flights. Who shall his fame impair
When thou art dead, and all thy wretched crew?

And so 'The First Fab Four', as they could quite reasonably be termed, came together for the first time, not, admittedly, as closely as their successors, but certainly as united in spirit and intention. Over the next decade they would interact as peers, inspiring and irritating each other but with a common project as focused as that of the Beatles, to contribute to what Shelley called 'that great poem, which all poets, like the co-operating thoughts of one great mind, have built up since the beginning of time'.

The next and last time that they would be so unified would be on a beach in Italy, nearly ten years later, in a performance that would go down in history as powerfully as The Beatles' last rooftop concert at 3 Savile Row in London.

5

Two of us: Hunt and Byron in England

When Hunt and his brother John were released in February 1815 they continued their work on *The Examiner*, which they had been able to keep publishing from their prison cells. Hunt retained a political stance in his essays and opinion pieces but introduced a wider, longer-term approach. 'If the political scene seemed grim' he wrote, 'one could still fight the good fight through a process of cultural education: one might not be able to change the government in the next election but one could educate the next generation in a broader, more liberal view'.

He had taken an apartment in Maida Vale, and after his two-year spell in prison was reluctant to go out on visits, asking that friends dropped in on him instead. Byron was one of his visitors: it was the best time in their relationship. Hunt's position as poet, activist and editor, and the credibility gained though his imprisonment meant that he more than held Byron's attention, while Hunt was impressed not only with Byron's rank and status as the best-selling poet of the day but also with his impressive appearance and no doubt fascinating conversation. Byron offered him free seats at Drury Lane theatre (where he was on the board of governors) but Hunt declined them, no doubt fearing his critical impartiality might be affected.

When Hunt was working on 'The Story of Rimini' in his decorated prison room, Byron had brought him books that he thought might help him with the task, and now, in

Maida Vale, Hunt showed him the results. Though admiring Hunt's political stance, he was less impressed by his poetic style, and going through Hunt's manuscript of the poem he made 'tactful expressions in the margins for the deletion of some precious expressions'. As he wrote later, 'When I saw Rimini in MS, I told him I deemed it good poetry at bottom, disfigured only by a strange style'. His answer was, that his style was a system, or *upon system,* or some such cant; and, when a man talks of system, his case is hopeless…'

Later, after Hunt had moved to Hampstead and completed it, Byron not only praised it highly (despite noting the 'occasional quaintness and obscurity' of some of its language), but even, in November 1815, recommended it to his own publisher John Murray. It 'was the safest thing you ever engaged in. I speak to you as a man of business; were I to talk to you as a reader or a critic, I should say it was a very wonderful and beautiful performance, with just enough of a fault to make its beauties more remarked and remarkable'.

For his part, Leigh Hunt came to Byron's defence when news began circulating in London that his marriage to Annabella Milbanke was running into difficulties. There were rumours that Byron was involved in unspeakable activities such as 'criminal intercourse', 'unnatural crimes' and incest with his half-sister Augusta. So he visited Byron at his London home to hear a not entirely ringing defence: out of the 'fifty reports' relating to his alleged misconduct, 'it follows that forty-nine must have more or less error or exaggeration'. Yet he added that he thought a separation 'inevitable'.

When Byron's wife walked out on him in January 1816, and just before Byron left the country in April, Hunt commented on the affair in an article titled 'Distressing Circumstances in High Life' referring to 'reckless calumniators' who 'know nothing of the matter' and who had 'brought out the vilest accusations' about it. What was more, he continued, Byron 'possesses qualities which ought to crumble the consciousness of these men to dust'.

Later Byron would tell Shelley's cousin Tom Medwin: 'When party feeling ran high against me, Hunt was the only editor, the only literary man, who dared say a word in my justification. I shall always be grateful for the part he played on that occasion'.

Byron's dramatic departure from England, bursting the bubble of high society adulation, was a foreshadowing of the furore that surrounds contemporary celebrity scandals and break-ups. Not only was there intense media interest, but he was pursued by bailiffs as well, and there were desperate attempts to catch a glimpse of the poet. At Dover 'The curiosity to see him was so great that many ladies accoutred themselves as chambermaids for the purpose of obtaining under that disguise a nearer inspection while he continued at the inn...'

And there was, of course, Byron's poem 'Fare thee well', originally written for Annabella but a work that unsurprisingly had found its way into the popular press.

Fare thee well! and if for ever,
Still for ever, fare thee well:
Even though unforgiving, never
'Gainst thee shall my heart rebel.

Wordsworth called it doggerel, and its author 'insane'; maliciously, he encouraged a newspaper editor (John Scott of *The Champion*) to redouble and increase his attacks on Byron, adding to the campaign of vilification against him. The wits of the day had their fun too: Thomas Love Peacock, in his novel 'Nightmare Abbey', satirised Byron in the figure of Mr Cypress who tells the Shelley figure (Scythrop):

'Sir, I have quarrelled with my wife; and a man who has quarrelled with his wife is absolved from all duty to his country. I have written an ode to tell the people as much, and they may take it as they list'.

And there was a flurry of poems on the subject of Byron's departure, an example of which, 'To Lord Byron', was published in the *Lady's Magazine* later in the year. As Byron was the 'much-injured' party, his loving and virtuous wife, unable to let him wander in loneliness, soon would 'fold him to her heart':

Fare thee well, much injured Byron!
Driven from thy native shore;
Ev'ry heart, save hearts of iron,
Deep must thy sad fate deplore.

Who unmov'd could hear those numbers
Tun'd to her thy soul ador'd?
Ev'n in breasts where pity slumbers
They might strike a tender chord.

Can she, then, the cause of anguish,
  She whose virtues all excel,—
Can she suffer thee to languish,
  Nor her dire resentment quell?

Will she let thee, broken-hearted,
  Wander on a foreign shore?
From each valued friend departed,
  Love and friendship known no more!

None to rouse thy soul-fix'd sadness,—
  None to watch thy fev'rish rest,
Soothe the thought that groans to madness
  In thy too high-swelling breast!

No — a woman's bosom tender
  Cannot bear so stern a part;
Soon her anger will surrender—
  Soon she'll fold thee to her heart.

Not everyone was so sympathetic, as the not-so-pithily titled 'Impromptu Address to Lord Byron, on reading his last Production of 'Fare thee Well'; being an humble Imitation of Dr. Johnson's celebrated Apostrophe', published in the *Morning Post* in April 1816, made clear:

Would'st thou had virtue more,
  Or that thou could'st not write;
For nought's so past enduring,

43

As a learned Hypocrite.
Fare thee well!

Hunt published in *The Examiner* his own contribution to the poetic commentary on Byron's departure – 'To the right honourable Lord Byron on his Departure for Italy and Greece, a verse Epistle', which began:

Since you resolve, dear BYRON, once again
To taste the far-eyed freedom of the main,
And as the coolness lessens in the breeze,
Strike for warm shores that bathe in classic seas,—
May all that hastens, pleases, and secures,
Fair winds and skies, and a swift ship, be yours...

It demonstrated Hunt's good nature, but also, as Robert Gittings put it, 'the splendid absurdities from which Hunt's poetry was seldom free...' Keats, having just received an encouraging note from Hunt about his poem 'To Solitude', was inclined to be impressionable, and 'took in his stride Hunt's picture of the Mediterranean full of bathing beauties, white and shapely, assembled there for Byron's benefit, 'To hail the laurell'd bard, that goes careering by'.

On 25th April 1816 his loyal friend Hobhouse waved him off from the quay, and wrote: 'God bless him for a gallant spirit and a kind one...' Amid this cacophony of scandal, shockingly bad poems, rumour, public curiosity, cartoons, caricatures and controversy, Byron crashed out of public life in Britain, never to return. For the moment he had bowed out of Hunt's life too, but Keats and then Shelley were about to make their entrances.

6

Goodbye, Hello

So Lord Byron would bid goodbye to life in England in early 1816; the rest of the year would see increasing ties between the Younger Romantics. Shelley would meet Byron and begin a lifelong association; Keats and Shelley would meet through Leigh Hunt, beginning an important but somehow disappointing friendship.

In terms of parallels between The Beatles Keats would have his own 'Aunt Mimi' moment – 'A guitar's alright John, but you'll never make a living from it'; Mary Shelley would create a character and a myth in 'Frankenstein' that would find its way into the Beatles story; Shelley would not only outrage the Bible Belt of his day as John Lennon did with his 'The Beatles are bigger than Jesus' remark but would also abandon his wife as John Lennon abandoned Cynthia. Hunt would play Brian Epstein by introducing both Keats and Shelley to a wider audience.

At the beginning of the year Keats was attending lectures at Guy's hospital. He was still dressing like Byron, reading Hunt's *Examiner* with its eulogies to the now-exiled Byron, and realising that there could be an opening for contributions from unpublished poets. Accordingly he submitted his Wordsworth-influenced sonnet 'To Solitude' to the editor, to find that, disappointingly, it was not published in the next edition of 28th April. However, there was a little note: 'J.K., and other Communications, next week'. And so, in the next issue of *The Examiner*, thanks to Leigh Hunt, he became a published poet. 'He was exceedingly gratified' one of fellow students, Henry Stephens wrote, and faced with the dilemma of following his heart through poetry or his head through medicine he settled on a middle way. He would write as much as possible but keep his irons in the medical fire for the moment.

As Keats was preparing for his exams that summer, the 23-year-old Shelley met Lord Byron on the shores of Lake Geneva, an encounter enabled by Mary Shelley's step-sister Claire Clairmont. She had linked up romantically with Byron in his final summer in London, and now had 'scrambled six hundred miles to unphilosophize me' as Byron put it.

It could be compared with another famous meeting, that of John Lennon and Paul McCartney at the Woolton church fete. John had impressed Paul by performing in The Quarrymen and adlibbing the words to the doo-wop classic 'Come Go With Me'. Paul had then impressed John by playing him a deft version of Eddie Cochrane's 'Twenty Flight Rock' in the church hall – as well as showing him how to tune his guitar properly. Both were clearly to be reckoned with.

As were Byron and Shelley. Byron's fame and notoriety could not be ignored, and the young author of the subversive, visionary 'Queen Mab' made Byron's posturings seem a little hollow. Though they complained about each other behind their backs (with Byron griping about Shelley's 'Wordsworth physic' and Shelley declaring that 'Lord Byron is an exceedingly interesting person, and as such it is to be regretted that he is a slave to the vilest and most vulgar prejudices, and as mad as the winds'), they would build on their relationship over the summer.

And so their friendship began, just as Lennon and McCartney's got underway after their church hall meeting. Though John Lennon saw McCartney as an equal and possible rival ('I had to decide whether to make myself stronger or make the group stronger'), he eventually decided on the latter. So their partnership, that would merge their talents more closely than Byron and Shelley could ever achieve, began.

With the Villa Diodati rented by Byron, the Shelley household staying nearby, and in an eerie atmosphere caused by the worldwide effects of a volcanic explosion in Indonesia, the scene was set for one of the great moments in English literature. The 19-year-old Mary Shelley, then Mary Godwin, outshone both Shelley and Byron in a ghost story writing contest to produce a book that landed perfectly in a society being shaken up by the ongoing march of science – the modern myth of 'Frankenstein'. Her moment of inspiration came one night: 'I saw—with shut eyes, but acute mental vision,—I saw the pale student of unhallowed arts kneeling beside the thing he had put together. I saw the hideous phantasm of a man stretched out, and then, on the working of some powerful engine, show signs of life, and stir with an uneasy, half vital motion'.

The fact that Frankenstein's monster features in the Beatles' animated film 'Yellow Submarine' demonstrates the longevity of her creation. In the film, Ringo and Young Fred, the refugee from Pepperland, open one of the doors in the 'House of the Beatles' to find the monster secured to a table. When Ringo pulls a lever ('I'm a born lever-puller, me') it stretches, burst its bonds, drinks something from a test tube – and turns into John. Her nineteenth century nightmare had made its way from a 3-volume inexpensively bound novel published in 1818 to become part of 20th century pop culture. At a stroke Mary Shelley had become the First Lady of the Romantics, bringing to them, like Yoko Ono with The Beatles, a significant female artistic presence.

Of course, at this point in Switzerland she was not Mary Shelley at all, but Mary Wollstonecraft Godwin, daughter of philosopher William Godwin and feminist pioneer Mary Wollstonecraft. Like Yoko Ono, she had displaced a previous partner from a failing marriage; for Shelley her love came as an overwhelming release from a failing marriage, a 'rash and heartless union' as he had come to describe it. Now Mary had fulfilled the human 'thirst for communion', which he saw as not merely of the senses but of 'our whole nature, intellectual, imaginative and sensitive'. And so he wrote:

> No more alone through the world's wilderness,
>   Although I trod the paths of high intent,
> I journeyed now: no more companionless…

As one Shelley scholar put it: Shelley had 'discovered in his second wife not simply a new fund of sympathy but an active feminine intelligence equal and complementary to his own' – could there be a more perfect description of John Lennon's own discovery, in Yoko Ono, of his own corresponding companion and fellow spirit? So his personal journey had been the same as Shelley's, and was fulfilled in the same way by Yoko, who had appeared 'out the blue', as he put it on his 1973 album 'Mindgames', and satisfied those deeper needs that Shelley had identified.

As it happens there is a spot in London where the paths of the two couples, Shelley and Mary, and John Lennon and Yoko Ono, overlap.

In the high summer of 1968, on July 28th to be precise, the Beatles visited St Pancras Old Church and Gardens on their 'Mad Day Out', in the process taking the photographs which grace the inner cover of their 'Blue' 1967-1970 compilation album. They had photographers in tow, fans homing in on them, and a new face in the Beatles group – Yoko Ono. Unbeknown to them John and Yoko were treading the same ground as Shelley and Mary, who had visited the churchyard at the onset of their relationship. It was here, by the grave of her mother Mary Wollstonecraft, that Mary had declared her love for him, and, in that moment of truth, Shelley knew his marriage to Harriet was over.

The comparable moment in John and Yoko's story – 'when we locked eyes and she got it and I got it' – had taken place over eighteen months earlier at the Indica Gallery in Mason's Yard, but that would set in train a process that would lead to John and Cynthia's divorce. The beautiful and blameless Cynthia would live on till 2015; for Harriet, Shelley's forsaken wife, things would take a more tragic turn.

While Mary started putting a structure and a plot to 'Frankenstein', Byron was completing a third canto of 'Childe Harold', and after visiting the Castle of Chillon with Shelley (on a boat trip round Lake Geneva that would cement their friendship), wrote his meditation on liberty and oppression 'The Prisoner of Chillon'. He began 'Manfred' with its doomed and defiant hero, which would become 'one of the most popular and influential literary works of the nineteenth century'. In addition, influenced by the unusually gloomy weather he completed his poem 'Darkness'. He recalled that 'I wrote it... at Geneva, when there was a celebrated dark day, on which the fowls went to roost at noon, and the candles were lighted as at midnight'.

> I had a dream, which was not all a dream.
> The bright sun was extinguish'd, and the stars
> Did wander darkling in the eternal space,
> Rayless, and pathless, and the icy earth
> Swung blind and blackening in the moonless air;
> Morn came and went and came, and brought no day,
> And men forgot their passions in the dread
> Of this their desolation; and all hearts
> Were chill'd into a selfish prayer for light....

It was an apocalyptic vision of a world without light and heat, a forewarning for our age of the fragility of humanity and its planet home. Amongst other things it warns us that the label 'Romantic', with its suggestions of the starry-eyed, impractical, quixotic etc., has to be treated with some caution. It was an unsparing vision: the creator God is not there to ride to the rescue, and Nature is not the kindly force that Wordworth would take it for. His pronouncement in 'Tintern Abbey': 'Nature never did betray/The heart that loves her' could not get past Byron's tough-minded muse.

That summer Shelley created a furore comparable to that following John Lennon's offhand comment that 'The

Beatles are more popular than Jesus now'. On the walking tour into the mountains that would inspire his poem 'Mont Blanc', and on opening a hotel register to check in, he found that the previous guest had written in his entry something like 'No one can look on these magnificent mountains without being convinced of the existence of God'. The iconoclastic Shelley immediately showed that actually, somebody could, and in the hotel register, in the occupation column, wrote in Greek 'I am a lover of mankind and an atheist' and gave his destination as 'L'Enfer'.

'Why do you call yourself an atheist?' he was asked later in Pisa. 'It annihilates you in this world'. The hotel incident certainly was a defining moment in the creation of his public image. Shelley's scandalous entry was reported in the London press with a riposte 'If an atheist a fool – if not, a liar' and it would be noted also by the future poet laureate Robert Southey and used in subsequent hostile press reviews of his work. It also featured in one of the comments on his death: 'So Shelley, the great atheist, has gone down by water to eternal hellfire. Now he knows whether there is a God or not'.

Yet in both cases there is a sense that the outrage underestimated both Lennon and Shelley. The line from the Bible about how people flocked to Jesus: 'And they came to him from all quarters' applied equally to the Beatles, and Lennon was making an intuitive observation, from his unique perspective, about movement in human history, about the deep charisma that moves the human spirit. Perhaps the rise of the charismatic rock star in the 20th century has shone a revealing backwards light into the history of religion, showing something of the human qualities that had animated the initiators of the world's major belief systems.

As for Shelley, he had argued in his notes to 'Queen Mab' that the grandeur of Nature does not amount to an argument for a Creator God: 'The plurality of worlds, the indefinite immensity of the universe is a most awful subject of contemplation. He who rightly feels its mystery and grandeur is in no danger of seductions from the falsehoods of religious systems or of deifying the principle of the universe'.

Both Shelley and Lennon had their own spiritual approaches, with Shelley conceding that a 'pervading Spirit coeternal with the universe' was at least a possibility and Lennon declaring in one of his last interviews that he 'certainly wasn't an atheist'. Perhaps Shelley's definition of 'what men call God' is the best fit for them both: 'the interfused and overruling Spirit of all the energy and wisdom within the circle of existing things'.

With the summer coming to an end Shelley and his household returned to England, with a number of unborn children, both metaphorical and actual. There was the manuscript of the third canto of 'Childe Harold' to deliver to John Murray, there was the unfinished manuscript of Mary's 'Frankenstein', and there was also the pregnant Claire Clairmont, four months into her term with the child conceived with Byron. For the moment Shelley had committed to looking after the baby as part of his household, an offer which could expose him to another level of character assassination. Back in England they took up lodgings in Bath.

The summer in Switzerland and the meeting with Byron had generated a lifelong friendship for Shelley. In Byron's conversation and companionship that summer he had found a 'light of enchantment that can never be dissolved'. The two were bound together by background and similar circumstances: both could have gone into conventional politics but both had found that poetry was their vocation. Shelley could provide direction to his fellow poet, who had stumbled naturally into 'scribbling verses' but lacked his own belief in its social value. After witnessing Byron's prolific gift he had suggested it could be best expressed in some kind of epic poem. Though Byron demurred, Shelley's proposal would eventually be realised in 'Don Juan'.

Meanwhile, 'fresh fields and pastures new' were opening up for John Keats, largely thanks to Leigh Hunt. Since Hunt's release from prison Charles Cowden Clarke, the son of Keats's Enfield headmaster and Keats's friend and supporter, had got increasingly friendly with him, as well as encouraging Keats in his ambitions. He would discuss Hunt's poetry, including his 'Story of Rimini', with him – a mixed blessing as Hunt, as Byron had complained, was adopting an idiosyncratic and affected theory of poetry.

Keats was known to Hunt as the author of the sonnet 'To Solitude', which he had published earlier in the year. In October John Keats himself had arrived at Hunt's new residence, a cottage on Hampstead Heath, bringing some more recent poems including his first poem of fulfilled genius 'On First Looking into Chapman's Homer'.

Much have I travell'd in the realms of gold,
And many goodly states and kingdoms seen;
Round many western islands have I been
Which bards in fealty to Apollo hold.
Oft of one wide expanse had I been told
That deep-brow'd Homer ruled as his demesne,
Yet did I never breathe its pure serene
Till I heard Chapman speak out loud and bold:
Then felt I like some watcher of the skies
When a new planet swims into his ken;
Or like stout Cortez when with eagle eyes
He stared at the Pacific, and all his men
Look'd at each other with a wild surmise,
Silent, upon a peak in Darien.

As Paul Gallagher has said, the significance of 'Chapman's Homer' for Keats was that it liberated Homer from the 'mathematizing' language he so detested. Keats had only read Homer in Pope's translation; now he saw a radically different version. Chapman, a contemporary of Shakespeare, had translated a section of Homer's 'Odyssey' where Odysseus emerges, half-drowned, from the sea as:

Then forth he came, his both knees faltering, both
His strong hands hanging down, and all with froth
His cheeks and nostrils flowing, voice and breath
Spent to all use, and down he sank to death.

How it contrasted, for Keats, with Pope's lifeless rendering:

From mouth and nose the briny torrent ran,
And lost in lassitude lay all the man,
Deprived of voice, of motion, and of breath;
The soul scarce waking in the arms of death.

'I shall never forget the impression made upon me by the exuberant specimens of genuine though young poetry that were laid before me' Hunt recalled. 'We became friends on the spot, and I found the young poet's heart as warm as his imagination'. The meeting had been engineered by Charles Cowden Clarke, and he remembered that the initial meeting 'stretched into three morning calls' and that 'Keats was suddenly made a familiar of the household'. 'We read and we talked together', Hunt remembered, 'and used to write verse of an evening upon a given subject'.

For Keats, who had been reading Hunt in *The Examiner* since his schooldays, this was a wonderful encounter with an admired figure and a well-connected professional writer and poet. His social horizons broadened dramatically with introductions to friends of Hunt including Godwin, Hazlitt, Shelley, his first publisher Charles Ollier, the now largely forgotten poet Barry Cornwall, and Wordsworth. In short, Keats's meeting with Hunt led to a sea-change in his life, and he expressed his delight in one of the poems he wrote that autumn, 'Keen, fitful gusts…'

For I am brimfull of the friendliness
That in a little cottage I have found…

It was at Hunt's Hampstead cottage that Shelley, Hunt and Keats all became acquainted with each other. By his standards the year of 1816 had not been creatively fruitful for Shelley, but he had written his 'Hymn to Intellectual

Beauty' in Switzerland, and this he had sent to Hunt – who had promptly lost the manuscript. However, their correspondence continued, and their relationship strengthened further when, on 1st December Leigh Hunt published a piece in *The Examiner* entitled 'Young Poets'. After mentioning Lord Byron and the third canto of 'Childe Harold's Pilgrimage', he described Shelley as a 'a very striking and original thinker', and promised to publish his 'Hymn' in the next issue.

Hunt mentioned Keats's friend John Hamilton Reynolds, and then wrote: 'The last of these young aspirants… is JOHN KEATS. He has not yet published anything except in a newspaper; but a set of his manuscripts were handed to us the other day, and fairly surprised us with the truth of their ambition, and ardent grappling with nature'. After putting 'On first looking into Chapman's Homer' into print for the first time, he quibbled about the phrase 'realms of gold' but pronounced it 'excellent', with a 'powerful and quiet' conclusion.

Hunt's article gave Keats heart and confirmed him on his poetic path. For a second time Keats's fellow student Henry Stephens (who went on to found the Stephens ink company) was there to leave a comment: 'This sealed his fate'. For Keats then made the momentous decision to abandon medicine as a career.

In December 1816 Shelley visited Hunt in Hampstead, and there met his fellow poet. From the beginning there was a distance between the two. As Hunt remembered, 'Keats did not take to Shelley as kindly as Shelley did to him'. He attributed the awkwardness between them to a number of factors: 'Keats, being a little too sensitive on the score of his origin, felt inclined to see in every man of birth a sort of natural enemy. Their styles of writing also were very different; and Keats … was so far inferior in universality to his great acquaintance that he could not accompany him in his daedal rounds with nature and his Archimedean endeavours to move the globe with his own hands'.

In addition, Shelley's new friendship with Hunt threatened to overpower his own. When, that very month, a young woman's body, that of Shelley's abandoned wife Harriet, was found in the Serpentine in Hyde Park it sparked a huge personal crisis for Shelley which could not but overshadow Hunt's rapport with Keats. He had stood by Byron after his marriage had ended; now he stood by Shelley when this tragedy with all its implications crashed over him. At the height of the personal sense of shock, when Shelley had just heard the news, he wrote to Mary: 'Leigh Hunt has been with me all day, and his delicate and tender attentions to me, his kind speeches of you, have sustained me against the weight of the horror of this event'.

Harriet, pregnant and since adolescence prone to suicidal thoughts, could have reorientated herself (young ladies of good families like her could leave town and have their child out of the sight of a censorious social set-up). Despite this, she was in a very difficult position. Abandoned by her husband, neglected by her family, with that weight of social disapproval weighing on her and living alone in lodgings in Knightsbridge, she had taken what seemed the only route possible.

Harriet's life had ended in tragedy; one and a half centuries later Cynthia managed to rebuild her life despite feeling that her former existence would always overshadow her. One can only be thankful for the changes in attitudes and legislation since then that have led to greater freedoms for women and greater opportunities to navigate new personal waters.

By this time the newly qualified Keats was apparently set for a career in surgery. He was working as a dresser to a notoriously clumsy surgeon called Lucas, the despair of his fellow surgeons, prone to cutting into arteries instead of opening a vein. Keats sometimes assisted, but was finding that his mistakes, and those of others at the hospital, were increasingly preying on his mind. He was also losing concentration at lectures, and realising that the surgeon's life was not for him. He told a friend later: 'My last operation was the opening of a man's temporal artery. I did it with the utmost nicety; but, reflecting on what passed through my mind at the time, my dexterity seemed a miracle, and I never took up the lancet again'.

Following the deaths of his parents a guardian, Richard Abbey had been appointed to manage the money that had been left in trust for him. Thinking that Keats would be well-served by a medical career, he had invested from Keats family funds to see him through his training. Now, with Keats having reached his 21st birthday, having become a full 'Licentiate of the Society of Apothecaries', and also having come into full possession of his inheritance, he had decided to propose that he set up a practice in or around Edmonton where the Keats family had local connections.

At the end of December Abbey duly 'communicated his plans to his ward, but his surprise was not moderate, to hear in reply, that he did not intend to be a Surgeon – Not intend to be a Surgeon! Why what do you mean to be? I mean to rely on my Abilities as a Poet – John, you are either mad or a Fool, to talk in so absurd a Manner. My mind is made up said the youngster very quietly. I know that I possess Abilities greater than most Men, and therefore I am determined to gain my Living by exercising them'.

Aunt Mimi's celebrated advice to the young John Lennon was very like Abbey's own conclusion: 'Seeing nothing could be done [he] called him a Silly Boy, & prophesied a speedy Termination to his inconsiderate enterprise'. As will be seen, in John Keats's case the hard-headed advice of the realist, in worldly, or strictly financial terms at least, proved to be right. It would only be years after his death that his work would find an audience.

As the year of 1816 was coming to its close, the Younger Romantics' storyline was moving on. Keats had again been published in *The Examiner*, Shelley's 'Hymn to Intellectual Beauty' was in the pipeline. Byron's third canto of 'Childe Harold' was renewing bonds with his readership, tugging on their heartstrings with his opening reference to his daughter and his description of the ball in Brussels the night before Waterloo. Shelley's proselytising for Wordsworth had paid off in the passages where Byron took his hero through the Rhine valley and on to Switzerland:

> Are not the mountains, waves, and skies, a part
> Of me and of my soul, as I of them?
> Is not the love of these deep in my heart
> With a pure passion?

It certainly impressed a young lady in Virginia, Harriet by name, who contributed a 'Sonnet, written after reading the third Canto of Lord Byron's Childe Harold's Pilgrimage' to the *American Beacon*, in Norfolk, Virginia, in February 1817:

> Byron! Thy very soul is poetry,
> And as I read thy burning lines, I feel
> My heart within my throbbing bosom reel,
> And fast tears bathe my cheeks and fill mine eye.
> Byron! Thine eye "in a fine phrenzy" rolls,
> But 'tis a jaundic'd eye, and yellow seem
> All objects to its joy-withering beam,
> Yet has it magic power o'er kindred souls.
> Byron! Thou canst not die, while song shall live...'

Clearly Byron had his own young female fan base, as devoted as the girls outside the Plaza Hotel who would scream for The Beatles nearly 150 years later. Wordsworth, however, was not so taken, as Thomas Moore later recorded:

'Spoke of Byron's plagiarisms from him; the whole third canto of Childe Harold founded on his style and sentiments. The feeling of natural objects which is there expressed, not caught by B. from nature herself, but from him

(Wordsworth), and spoiled in the transmission. Tintern Abbey the source of it all; from which same poem too the celebrated passage about Solitude, in the first canto of Childe Harold, is (he said) taken, with this difference, that what is naturally expressed by him, has been worked by Byron into a laboured and antithetical sort of declamation'.

Byron may have left Britain in disgrace, but the new canto of 'Childe Harold' was an eloquent response from exile. It was a distinct advance on the first two, more mature, more accomplished poetically, and with its new directly personal tone, developing his relationship with his readership. He was showing himself as adept as any major star in managing his own image, with an awareness of his audience and the psychological needs that they projected onto him.

So 1816 had been a momentous, formative period in the young poets' lives. It ended with the publication of another best-selling Byron edition, 'The Prisoner of Chillon and other poems', which included 'Darkness'. John Keats was reflecting on his new friendships with his sonnet 'Great Spirits Now on Earth Are Sojourning' declaring that a new poetic generation 'will give the world another heart, And other pulses…. Listen awhile ye nations, and be dumb'.

On the penultimate day of the year Shelley and Mary were married in St Mildred's Church, Bread Street, London.

7

A Year in the Life

On 14th April 1965 the Beatles drove down a suburban road in South London, Ailsa Road in Twickenham to be precise, and disembarked from their Rolls Royce to open four adjacent front doors. They were filming their second movie 'Help!' of course, and they entered one large interior room set up perfectly to reflect their inseparability as well as their distinctive personalities. While George interacted with a mysterious gardener, John extracted 'A Spaniard in the Works' from a revolving bookcase and settled into a sunken reading spot, Paul rose from an underground room playing a glowing Wurlitzer organ, and Ringo selected a sandwich from his very own dispensing machine.

Almost exactly 150 years previously, across the river in north London in 1817, the Vale of Health in Hampstead to be precise, stood the little cottage where Leigh Hunt lived, with its own idiosyncratic aura. It was, perhaps, a 19th century equivalent of the Beatles' house – a poet's house, adorned with casts of poets from the ages – and as Shelley would remember, 'With graceful flowers tastefully placed about, And coronals of bay from ribbons hung, And brighter wreaths in neat disorder flung....'

Keats, who had a bed made up for him in Hunt's library during his visits, devoted 50 lines of 'Sleep and Poetry to describing it and its contents, recording 'Sappho's meek head … half smiling down', 'Great Alfred's too, with anxious, pitying eyes', 'Kosciusko's worn/By horrid suffrance—mightily forlorn' and 'Petrarch, outstepping from the shady green'. Scattered manuscripts and unrestrained children added to the bohemian atmosphere, and it was a centre for supper parties, picnics, and theatre outings.

In this environment, Hunt and Shelley's friendship was deepening, and in the New Year, in January 1817 Hunt finally published Shelley's 'Hymn to Intellectual Beauty' in *The Examiner*. The poem, beginning:

> The awful shadow of some unseen Power
> Floats through unseen among us,—visiting
> This various world with as inconstant wing
> As summer winds that creep from flower to
> flower…

demonstrated how the Romantics foreshadowed The Beatles' own spiritual characteristics, based in loose pantheistic and humanistic values (seen in songs like 'Tomorrow never Knows', 'Across the Universe' and 'Because').

With its publication Shelley now had an entrée to London literary life, and a greater degree of credibility – all his previous poems and pamphlets had been self-published. While Keats did not particularly care for the 'Hymn', he did appreciate its quality of the work, and it did perhaps have a subconscious effect on one of his greatest poems, 'To Autumn', written three years later. For one of the passages in Shelley's poem reads:

> The day becomes more solemn and serene
> When noon is past; there is a harmony
> In autumn, and a lustre in its sky,
> Which through the summer is not heard or seen,
> As if it could not be, as if it had not been!

Perhaps this was somewhere in Keats's consciousness three years later in Winchester, when he wrote 'To Autumn'. In the same way it's quite possible that the John Lennon line from 'I am the Walrus', on being in an English garden, and waiting for the sun, was in George Harrison's when the opening line of 'Here comes the Sun' came to him.

There was clearly something very special about the creative chemistry engendered by the closeness of The Beatles. A recent revelation in the 'Get Back' films was of John bluntly telling George that the waltz-based tune he had just brought in ('I Me Mine') would not do for a rock band like The Beatles; when eventually recorded it would include a rock chorus that could have resulted from Lennon's criticism. That type of interaction, inviting creative response, helped them reach a level of attainment that was only intermittently achieved in their later solo careers.

Though the Romantics were working as individuals rather than in a group they still fed off each other creatively, similarly inviting each other into new territories. One poem Keats produced, 'Written in Disgust of Vulgar Superstition' had a distinctly Shelleyan air, and Shelley's longer poem 'Alastor' certainly intrigued him. Not only was its subject matter, a poet's search for beauty, of central interest to him but 'this complete and highly-finished work' was 'nearly twice as long as anything he himself had done'. Accordingly, spurred on by Shelley's achievement, he began to think in terms of publishing a collection of his own work. With the assistance of Hunt, Keats had been introduced to the publishers Charles and John Ollier, and in March his first book simply entitled 'Poems' appeared, opening with a dedication to Leigh Hunt which ended:

And I shall ever bless my destiny,
That in a time, when under pleasant trees
Pan is no longer sought, I feel a free,
A leafy luxury, seeing I could please
With these poor offerings, a man like thee.

The edition ended with 'Sleep and Poetry' (an 'ominous title' said Byron later), which contained a combative attack on what Keats saw as the formulaic poetry of the 18th century, dominated by the theories of Hobbes and the French poet Boileau. The poets of the previous century such as Pope and Dryden, who were still the arbiters of taste, were, according to Keats:

…closely wed
To musty laws lined out with wretched rule
And compass vile: so that ye taught a school
Of dolts to smoothe, inlay, and clip, and fit,
Till, like the certain wands of Jacob's wit,
Their verses tallied. Easy was the task:
A thousand handicraftsman wore the ma'k
Of Poesy….

On Saturday 1st March Keats was presumably on a high, having just received the first copy of his new book from the publishers. Immediately he set off from his lodgings in Cheapside to show it to Hunt in Hampstead. Unfortunately, because of Hunt, the triumphant 'show and tell' turned into an embarrassing situation of the first order. To celebrate the young poet's achievement Hunt made a wreath of laurel – the Greek symbol of victory and accomplishment – and wound it round Keats's head. Keats reciprocated, and in their congratulatory headgear, in Hunt's garden, they sat drinking and each completing a sonnet to a 15 minute deadline.

It was at this point that three young ladies walked in, the sisters of a mutual friend. Hunt took his wreath off, but Keats defiantly left his on – afterwards trying to write away his embarrassment with another poor sonnet 'To the ladies who saw me crown'd' and a longer, defensive 'Hymn to Apollo' which contains the line 'When like a blank idiot I put on thy wreath'.

What shook Keats was that Hunt 'proudly showed off both sonnets to all-comers, and to Keats's evident mortification, even published his own in *The Examiner*'. Although Hunt had been well-meaning he had not only offended Keats's sense of taste but had given his critics a powerful weapon to use against him.

Keats and Shelley now agreed to write a 4,000 word poem in friendly competition. In Keats's case the subject was that of the Greek myth of 'Endymion'; Shelley's epic was to be called 'Laon and Cythna', the story of a brother and sister who 'inspire and lead a bloodless revolution against the sultan of Turkey'. It would convey 'his vision of how the leaders ought to have conducted the French Revolution'. During the summer Shelley worked on his epic in Marlow, often writing on a boat on the river, while Keats left London for writing expeditions in the Isle of Wight, Margate and lastly Oxford.

Hunt and Shelley's friendship was deepening, with regular socializing at Shelley's recently acquired house in Marlow and in Hampstead, and Mary Shelley and Hunt's wife Marianne were becoming close. As for Byron, though far removed in Italy, he still loomed large in Shelley's mind. In January Claire had given birth to a baby girl, and, as Shelley wrote, 'she continues to reside with us under a feigned name. But we are somewhat embarrassed about her. We are exposed to what remarks her existence is calculated to excite'. As Robert Gittings and Jo Manton put it, 'to have an unaccountable infant in their home plunged the Shelleys into difficulties. They said the little girl, initially named Alba but baptised later as Clara Allegra, was 'the child of a friend in London', but this fiction could not last forever'.

For Claire this experience 'of maternal love was an experience beyond her imagining'. It 'made her fearful of sending the little girl, as she knew she had promised, to live with Byron'. For two main reasons, the awkwardness of the little girl's place in Shelley's household and the social and material benefits that would go with being brought up Byron, she 'talked herself into handing her over to him'. As for Shelley, from now on he would forever be in the supremely awkward position of negotiating on Claire's behalf over Allegra, while trying to keep his friendship with Byron alive.

In July he wrote again to Byron about Allegra, also commenting on the newly published 'Manfred'. 'I have read Manfred with the greatest admiration. The same freedom from rules that marked the 3rd canto (of Childe Harold) and

'Chillon' is visible here... But it made me dreadfully melancholy...'

Shelley's letter also mentioned Hunt: 'Hunt has been with me here, and we have often spoken of you. Hunt is an excellent man, and has a great regard for you'. He also mentioned his intention 'to seek Italy' 'if the Chancellor should threaten to invade my domestic circle' – a reference to his fear that he might be ruled unfit to bring up his two children by Mary.

By the autumn of 1817 the group were spread between London (Keats and Hunt), Marlow (Shelley) and Venice (Byron). Hunt and Shelley had become kindred spirits, but the relationship between Keats and Hunt had cooled. Keats's visit to Oxford ('the finest city in the world' as he described it) as a guest of a new friend and trainee ordinand Benjamin Bailey, had further diminished Hunt's influence on Keats's language, and greatly broadened his general poetic viewpoint.

Despite this, Keats was firmly associated with him in the eyes of those who so vehemently opposed Hunt's poetics and politics. That October, a media storm broke over Leigh Hunt's head, with a clear threat that it would later envelop his so-called followers, both Keats and Shelley. In October *Blackwood's Magazine*, the Edinburgh-based competitor to the *Quarterly Review*, published an anonymous attack on Hunt under the pseudonym 'Z'. Written by the 23-year-old John Gibson Lockhart, the son-in-law of Sir Walter Scott, he was Scott's future biographer and determined to make a stand against reform-minded literature.

So his opening shot was to distinguish the vulgar Hunt from the patrician Byron, deploring Hunt's dedication of 'The Story of Rimini' – which he described as 'indecent and immoral' – to Byron. And the threat to attack Keats, with all its implications for the forthcoming 'Endymion', was there in the article's parting shot. Sensing journalistic gold dust, *Blackwood's* would publish seven more articles on what it had dubbed 'The Cockney School'. In time Hunt would respond that he could hardly object to being classed in a group that included Chaucer, Milton and Pope!

By October Shelley, who had been staying with Hunt in his house in Lisson Grove since September, was approaching publishers with the finished text of 'Laon and Cythna: or, the Revolution of the Golden City', and had also secured a publishing deal for Mary's 'Frankenstein'. Keats had arrived back from Oxford, nursing a mysterious condition – thought to be a venereal disease – for which he was taking mercury, and was finding that 'every Body seems at loggerheads'. He found that Shelley and Hunt grated on him, and noted that he had 'refused to visit Shelley (in Marlow) that I might have my own unfettered scope'.

Hunt was praising Shelley's completed poem and preparing to publish extracts in *The Examiner*, while disparaging the unfinished 'Endymion', once casually riffling through it and paying it scant attention. And so, Keats wrote, 'I am quite disgusted with literary men and will never know another except Wordsworth – no, not even Byron'.

The attack on the 'Cockney School' was troubling, and he described it to Bailey in Oxford in December. 'There has been a flaming attack on Hunt in the Edinburgh Magazine. I never read anything more virulent – accusing him of the greatest crimes, depreciating his Wife, his Poetry, his Habits, his Company, his Conversation. … I don't mind the thing much – but if he goes to such lengths with me as he has with Hunt I must infallibly call him to an Account if he is a human being …' Despite this, which hardly promised well for his own work and career, on November 28th he finished and dated the completed 'Endymion'.

Shelley meanwhile was publishing 'Laon and Cythna' through the Olliers, but had run into trouble: Laon and Cythna's relationship was so close to incestuous that a prosecution was likely. Shelley agreed to amend it, and as he wrote to Byron in December, 'my long poem under the title 'The Revolt of Islam' is almost printed'. In order to focus on its publication, and also to finalise details of bringing 'Frankenstein' to press, Shelley and Mary left the children in Marlow with Claire and moved into an apartment near the Euston Road, 19 Mabledon Place. There they were visited by Keats, in the company of the editor Walter Coulson.

As Byron was accepting responsibility for Allegra, Shelley now wrote filling him in on her progress. She had 'grown exquisitely beautiful ... and has become affectionate, and mild. She is William's playmate, who is so fond of her that he will be among the many sincere mourners at her departure. They sit on the floor together and amuse themselves in the most sociable way; little William putting more than half the raisins, etc., that are given to him into her mouth'. It was just a case of seeing her safely to Byron in Italy – did he have any suggestions? 'We should' he concluded, 'be extremely happy to hear how you are getting on, and what you are doing, whether you are yet in love, or have been out, or in again'. He concluded by enquiring after

'Childe Harold': 'We hear of the 4th and last Canto, but have not yet seen it'.

In creative terms Byron, in Venice, was breaking new ground. While finishing the last canto of 'Childe Harold' (for which he would demand the princely sum of £2,625), he had discovered a new rhyme scheme which would help him to fully release his personality into his work. 'With one stroke he freed himself from the fetters of British propriety and the 'Childe Harold manner', and something of the careless and relaxed realism of his letters invaded his verse'.

Another significant event in Byron's life at this time was his sale of Newstead Abbey for around £95,000, a transaction which would free him from the debt that had always hung over him, partly due to his own profligacy.

So at the end of 1817 the four poets were venturing into new creative and personal areas: Keats with 'Endymion' finished and preparing for its publication; Byron with a new poetic form discovered and inaugurated; Hunt ever more conscious of the challenges in maintaining a liberal voice after Lockhart's assault, and Shelley with 'The Revolt of Islam' to launch and the pressure for a move to Italy building.

A few days before the New Year Keats, still maintaining his distance from Shelley, wrote to his brother George, telling him that 'Shelley's poem is out, and there are words about it being objected to as much as his Queen Mab was. Poor Shelley, I think he has his quota of good qualities, in sooth la!' The same letter contained one of the 'splendid insights' that pepper Keats's letters, the idea of 'Negative Capability': 'that is when man is capable of being in uncertainties, Mysteries, doubts, without any irritable reaching after fact & reason…'

At roughly the same time, during the Christmas season, Shelley sat down with his friend Horace Smith, both a poet and a stockbroker, to write about the massive statue of Rameses II and other Egyptian finds that had recently been put on show at the British Museum. Shelley produced what Richard Holmes called 'the finest sonnet he ever wrote: harsh, dramatic and deeply expressive of his eternal hatred of tyranny and his brooding philosophical scepticism'. It has even been described as expressing the default position behind all English literature, that of speaking truth to power and looking for grander perspectives behind apparent realities. In addition to deftly summoning up a dictator's nightmare, it shows that despite all the reservations about craftsmanship writing you *can* sit down and deliberately produce something of real quality.

Ozymandias

I met a traveller from an antique land
Who said:—Two vast and trunkless legs of stone
Stand in the desert. Near them on the sand,
Half sunk, a shatter'd visage lies, whose frown
And wrinkled lip and sneer of cold command
Tell that its sculptor well those passions read
Which yet survive, stamp'd on these lifeless things,
The hand that mock'd'them and the heart that fed.
And on the pedestal these words appear:
"My name is Ozymandias, king of kings:
Look on my works, ye mighty, and despair!"
Nothing beside remains: round the decay

Of that colossal wreck, boundless and bare,
The lone and level sands stretch far away.

8

'I'll follow the Sun'

John Lennon left Britain on August 31st 1971, seeking greater personal and artistic freedom in America. He never returned to his homeland and would die in his newly adopted home. Percy Bysshe Shelley left the country on 13th March 1818, also never to return, and also suffering an untimely death, at a time when, as with John Lennon, new and fertile creative fields were ahead of him. Another factor that linked the two departures was shared concerns over children, with John and Yoko's attempt to locate Yoko's daughter Kyoto, who had been abducted by her father Tony Cox, influencing their decision to relocate to the USA.

After Harriet's suicide Lord Eldon, in the High Court, had ruled that Shelley was unfit to raise their two children, Charles and Ianthe, largely because of his authorship of 'Queen Mab'. Now he feared that a precedent had been set that could deprive him of his two children by Mary, William and Clara, as his verse 'To William', written shortly before boarding a boat to France showed:

> Come with me, thou delightful child,
> Come with me, though the wave is wild,
> And the winds are loose, we must not stay,
> Or the slaves of the law may rend thee away.
> They have taken thy brother and sister dear...

1818 would see the Younger Romantics divided between England and Italy. As Hunt carried on with *The Examiner* and embarked on new spin-offs, Keats would display his poetic ambition in 'Endymion' and begin work on the poems that would appear in 1820. In Venice Byron was working with the new poetic format that would go on to drive the epic, comic poem 'Don Juan', and Shelley would find in Italy a 'paradise of exiles' that would inspire his greatest work.

The opening months of 1818 saw the publication of Shelley's 'The Revolt of Islam'. Keats's epic 'Endymion' would see the light of day in early spring. Both poems are generally acknowledged to be problematic, but important to their authors' ultimate achievements. The ambition of both poets was plain to see.

Written with the aim of reviving a sense of idealism amongst British reformers in the wake of the failure of the French Revolution, 'The Revolt of Islam' was a complex allegorical tale in 12 cantos, describing how Cythna, followed by Laon, initiated a revolt against the tyrannical ruler of the fictional state of Argolis. It includes a beautiful dedication to Mary, and is penetrated by a sense of a cruel present and the looming possibilities of freedom.

Leigh Hunt had already printed a sizeable extract in November; in the new year he printed another and followed this with a favourable but not uncritical review. However, the reviews in other outlets were dismissive, passing over the poem's qualities and focusing on Shelley's private life and scandalous opinions. Byron, when he read the copy

Shelley had sent him, 'found it somewhat bewildering', though 'with much poetry in it'.

Hunt was less appreciative of Keats's 'Endymion'; in January Keats had written to George and Tom:

'Leigh Hunt I showed my 1st book to – he allows it not much merit as a whole; says it is unnatural and made ten objections to it in the mere skimming over…. The fact is that he and Shelley are hurt, and perhaps justly, at my not having shown them the affair officiously; and from several hints I have had they appear much disposed to dissect or anatomise any trip or slip I may have made - But who's afraid? Aye! Tom! Demme if I am.'

Keats sensed, perhaps unfairly, that Hunt and Shelley were ganging up on him, perhaps also realizing that he was continuing with a work he had already outgrown. Just how far he was moving on was seen when he completed a letter to John Hamilton Reynolds at the end of the month by announcing 'I will copy out my last sonnet….' There followed his beautiful meditation on mortality 'When I Have Fears', highlighting the fleeting preciousness of life.

On January 25th news came through that Shelley's house in Marlow had been sold, and the decision was made to move to Italy. At last Allegra could be delivered to Byron in Venice, and the Shelleys looked forward to cutting costs, escaping the possible consequences of Shelley's radical opinions and publications, and renewing their association with Byron. Visiting London on 4th February to begin the process of moving, Shelley spent the evening with Keats and Hunt; they sat down to each write a sonnet on the subject of the Nile. It was a bit like Lennon's comment that 'you want

a song about bananas for a movie? Sure, I'll do it but ....',
and as Richard Holmes puts it, while Hunt's version is
'competent ... both Keats's and Shelley's betray
embarrassment'.

His Lordship, meanwhile, was enjoying the Venice
carnival with all its spectacle and (no doubt) opportunities
for lovemaking, and was able to relax, with the final canto
of 'Childe Harold' and his new work 'Beppo' both
completed and submitted to John Murray for publication. He
should have been supremely confident and secure in his
fame and popular reach, but it was at this time that an
acquaintance recorded that 'Byron used to lament that he
could not versify as well as Shelley'.

At the end of February Murray published 'Beppo',
which was well received, with its humour and
conversational style winning over the critics. There was a
sense that Byron had finally found his true voice:

> With all its sinful doings, I must say,
> That Italy's a pleasant place to me…
>
> I love the language, that soft bastard Latin,
> Which melts like kisses from a female mouth…

In addition, there was a new self-deprecating tone:

> But I am but a nameless sort of person
> (A broken Dandy lately on my travels)
> And take for Rhyme, to hook my rambling Verse on,
> The first that Walker's Lexicon unravels,
> And when I can't find that, I put a worse on,
> Not caring as I ought for Critics' cavils;
> I've half a mind to tumble down to prose,
> But Verse is more in fashion–so here goes!

The story that Byron told in the poem was of a Venetian lady who takes a 'Cavaliere Servente' (a socially acceptable lover) after her husband had disappeared at sea, only to find that he reappears three years later, having been captured, enslaved, then freed by Turkish pirates. It gave Byron the chance to reflect on England, the differences between English and Italian moral attitudes, the position of women in Muslim societies – before winding up the story up with the husband's reconversion to Christianity and the restitution of his marriage:

> His Wife received, the Patriarch re-baptised him
> (He made the Church a present, by the way);
> He then threw off the Garments which disguised him
> And borrow'd the Count's small clothes for a day….

> …My pen is at the bottom of a page,
> Which being finish'd, here the story ends;
> 'Tis to be wish'd it had been sooner done,
> But Stories somehow lengthen when begun.

By the time it was published the Shelleys had left Marlow and moved to central London for their last weeks in England which saw the final meetings between Keats and Shelley. On March 11th he and his household left England on a stormy sea, writing to Hunt from Calais that they were all in high spirits. 'Motion always has this effect upon the blood, even when the mind knows that there are causes for dejection' he observed. Ten days later he wrote again: 'When shall I see you all again? Oh that it might be in Italy!'

Leigh Hunt had just published a new collection of poems 'Foliage', which included his poem to Byron, two dedicated to Shelley, and others to members of his Hampstead set of friends. From Lyons Shelley praised 'The Nymphs', the poem generally acknowledged to be the best of them, but gently criticized his friend's use of words: 'What a delightful poem The Nymphs is – especially the second part! It is truly poetical... If six hundred miles were not between us, I should say what a pity that 'glib' were not omitted, and the poem is not as faultless as it is beautiful...' Keats was in agreement; in a letter to Hunt written around a year earlier he had noted that it was weakened by some contrived phrases, and expressed the hope that he had cut phrases like 'unsuperfluous life', 'faint bowers', and 'fibrous roots'. Hunt, however, blithely paid no attention (after all, what did John Keats know about poetry?), and the lines made it through to publication. As for Byron, he was scathing about it; as Shelley noted later: 'He quizzes it immoderately'.

Keats's brother Tom had for some time been exhibiting alarming symptoms, and on doctor's orders had been ordered to spend the winter months on the South coast. Now Keats, at the beginning of March 1818, set off for Teignmouth to replace his brother George – who had signalled his intention to move to America to start a new life – as Tom's carer. He arrived, with the final part of 'Endymion' to fair copy, to find Tom spitting blood and looking pale and flushed alternately. The weather too was miserable: 'It is a splashy, rainy, misty, snowy, foggy, haily, floody, muddy slipshod County' he wrote, though 'the hills are very beautiful, when you get a sight of them....' Depressed by the situation he expressed doubt about his vocation as a poet and the value of poetry itself: 'I am sometimes so very sceptical as to think Poetry a mere Jack a lanthern to amuse whoever may chance to be struck with its brilliance'.

Nevertheless he finished his fair copy of 'Endymion', and after his first attempt at a preface had been rejected, sat down to write another. It was hardly a ringing endorsement, certainly not a clarion call, but it was honest, and expressed Keats's mature view on the poem. When published in early April its ambition and its 'gleams of genius' meant that it could not be entirely dismissed, with its first line in particular passing into, and permanently enriching, the English language. It even found its way into 'Yellow Submarine', with the Chief Blue Meanie parodying it by screeching: 'A thing of beauty. Destroy it forever!'

A thing of beauty is a joy for ever:
Its loveliness increases; it will never
Pass into nothingness; but still will keep
A bower quiet for us, and a sleep
Full of sweet dreams, and health, and quiet breathing.

However, the first review that appeared, in the *Quarterly Review*, was severe: 'This author is a copyist of Mr. Hunt; but he is more unintelligible, almost as rugged, twice as diffuse, and ten times more tiresome and absurd than his prototype....' And waiting in the wings, was someone with an even more serious amount of ill-will, sharpening his quill and waiting for the chance to renew his assault on 'The Cockney School'. Up in Edinburgh, Walter Scott's son-in-law John Wilson Lockhart saw 'Endymion' as nothing more than material for his ongoing polemic against Hunt and his circle.

At the end of April John Murray published the fourth and final canto of Byron's 'Childe Harold's Pilgrimage'. The poem was now nakedly autobiographical, with the persona of the wandering Harold dropped, and a more straightforward relationship with his readership assumed. Despite its famous beginning – 'I stood upon the Bridge of Sighs, a Palace and a Prison on each hand', and its moving personal declaration –

> But I have lived, and have not lived in vain;
> My mind may lose its force, my blood its fire…
> …But there is that within me which shall tire
> Torture and Time, and breathe when I expire
> Like the remembered tones of a mute lyre'

– the poem's treatment of his personal history relating to the breakup of his marriage and his exile has been criticised for its transparent lack of self-knowledge and its despairing view of human life. Peacock, who was completing a satirical novel based on Shelley and his circle, wrote to him in May:

'I have almost finished 'Nightmare Abbey. ' I think it necessary to 'make a stand' against the 'encroachments' of black bile. The fourth canto of 'Childe Harold' is really too bad. I cannot consent to be *auditor tantum* [only a listener] of this systematical 'poisoning' of the 'mind' of the 'reading public'.

And so, as Peter Cochran noted, 'Nightmare Abbey' contained a speech by Mr Cypress, the Byron character in the novel, made up entirely of quotes from the fourth canto:

'I have no hope for myself or for others. Our life is a false nature; it is not in the harmony of things; it is an all-blasting upas, whose root is earth, and whose leaves are the skies which rain their poison-dews upon mankind. We wither from our youth; we gasp with unslaked thirst for unattainable good; lured from the first to the last by phantoms – love, fame, ambition, avarice – all idle, and all ill – one meteor of many names, that vanishes in the smoke of death'.

To which Mr Flosky, the character drawn from Samuel Taylor Coleridge, replies:

'A most delightful speech, Mr. Cypress. A most amiable and instructive philosophy. You have only to impress its truth on the minds of all living men, and life will then, indeed, be the desert and the solitude ...'

The fourth canto fell foul of the Austrian authorities, as in stanzas 42 and 43 Byron had translated and adapted verses by the Italian patriotic poet Vincenzo da Filicaja which 'were banned in Italy under Austrian rule, a fact which Byron had learned in Switzerland'. When Michele Leoni produced a blank verse translation of the Canto and attempted to publish it in Italy, a letter was sent to Count

Sedinitsky, the head of Police in Vienna with a recommendation that it should be 'completely banned'. Subsequently the Italian edition of 'Childe Harold' was proscribed, and 'most of [Leoni's] print run destroyed'.

Meanwhile Shelley and Mary, together with their children William and Elena, as well as Claire and Allegra, not forgetting their Swiss maid Elise and English nurse Milly, had crossed into Italy with Shelley's library and its freethinking contents narrowly escaping confiscation at customs points along the way. Travelling down through the Alpine passes Shelley's spirits soared, and according to Claire he sang all the way, with one verse foreshadowing John Lennon's line – 'Imagine no religion':

> Now Heaven neglected is by men
> And gods are hung on every tree;
> But not the more for lack of them
> Shall this fair world unhappy be.

From Milan Allegra was despatched to Byron in Venice in the company of Elise, and the group, having failed to secure a lease on a house near Lake Como, set off via Pisa for Livorno, the home of John and Maria Gisborne, the latter of whom had nursed Mary Shelley after her mother's death. On their recommendation Shelley set off to locate a house for the summer in the spa town of Bagni di Lucca, in the foothills of the Apennines.

By midsummer the Shelleys were ensconced there in a spacious and well-maintained house, with Shelley devoting his time to translating Plato's 'Symposium'. Byron had leased part of a palazzo on the Grand Canal, the Palazzo

Mocenigo, and had brought Allegra there. In July he began working on a new poem, 'Don Juan', using Beppo's enticing metre, and was also finding the time to indulge a thoroughly dissolute lifestyle.

Though he had been away from England for over two years Hunt was still on his mind, and in a letter of 1st June 1818, just after moving into the Palazzo Mocenigo, he commented at length on Hunt, his 'system' of poetry, and his character in a letter to his friend Thomas Moore:

'Hunt … is a good man with some practical element in his chaos, but spoilt by the Christ Church Hospital and a Sunday newspaper to say nothing of the Surrey Gaol, which conceited him into a martyr...

…He believes his trash of vulgar phrases tortured into compound barbarisms to be *old* English … is an honest charlatan, who has persuaded himself into a belief of his own impostures….

But Leigh Hunt is a good man, and a good father – see his Odes to all the Masters Hunt; a good husband – see his sonnet to Mrs Hunt; - a good friend – see his epistles to various people; - and a great coxcomb and a very vulgar person in every thing about him. But that's not his fault, but of circumstances'.

Byron's opinions, voiced from his Italian exile, as well as Lockhart's polemics, are reminders that Hunt was still very much in the public's (and the poets') minds through his position at *The Examiner*, with its weekly commentary on politics and the arts. There was a keen demand for reformist literature, and Thomas Carlyle would remember the queue that would form every Sunday in his

Scottish village to await its arrival. Again and again, it would influence and inform especially Keats and Shelley ('Hunt as a political writer delights me more and more' wrote Shelley), and in many cases its reports would feed through into their work.

At the end of June Keats was on a coach to Liverpool, to see his brother George off to America. Even though he knew that he faced a drubbing from *The Quarterly*, and an onslaught from *Blackwood's*, his trip was a deliberate renewal of his poetic vocation, for he planned to gather material for a new work on a walking tour of Scotland. As he had put it: 'I intend within a Month to put a knapsack on my back and make a pedestrian tour through the north of England, and part of Scotland – to make a sort of Prologue to the Life I intend to pursue – that is, to see all of Europe at the lowest expense. I will clamber through the Clouds and exist'. He was doubling down on his ambition to be 'one of the English poets'.

Scotland was not only the land of Robert Burns (whose home was on the itinerary), but promised contact with epic scenery as well as encounters with the Scottish song tradition and the stories of Sir Walter Scott. So after seeing off George and his wife Georgiana, Keats and his friend Charles Brown took a coach to Lancaster, from where the walking tour would begin. They then walked into Westmorland, to find themselves surrounded by the maelstrom of the election where Wordsworth was supporting local landowner Lord Lowther against the reformer Henry Brougham.

After the polls had closed Keats called at Wordsworth's house in Ambleside, Mount Rydal, to find 'he was not at home nor any member of his family – I was much disappointed'. Brown remembered later 'the young poet looked thoughtful' when he learned that Wordsworth was with the Lowthers in Appleby, awaiting the result of the polls.

Shrugging off the disappointment and the reminder of his political differences with the older poet, Keats set out northwards, leaving the Lake District at the end of June and travelling to the Scottish border near Gretna Green by coach. However, while crossing the Isle of Mull, he 'caught a violent cold' and in Inverness a doctor concluded that he was 'too thin and weak to proceed'. Keats and Brown decided the walking tour had to be abandoned, and from the port of Cromarty, on August 8th, Keats set off alone for London. As Carol Kyros Walker put it, 'His condition was never quite the same afterwards. His defences were permanently down'.

Meanwhile, in Bagni di Lucca, Shelley, who had found himself 'incapable of original composition', continued working on the 'Symposium', Plato's amusing and insightful dialogue on the subject of love.

The calm of the summer months was broken by the arrival of two letters from Elise in Venice, bearing news that Allegra had been placed in the care of the British consul Richard Hoppner. Claire saw this as a violation of an agreement she had made with Byron in Switzerland, and her anxieties were increased by an alarming story that Elise had included. 'Lord Byron had been in the nursery … observing Allegrina at play. Of a sudden he said to the nurse 'She will grow up a very pretty woman and then I will take her for my mistress'. Elise then expressed shock, and Byron replied: 'I can very well do it – she is no child of mine – she is Mr Shelley's child'. The reliability of this is open to question, but what is certain is that the letters threw Claire into a panic, and she began pressing for an immediate visit to Venice. After some discussion Shelley decided to accompany her, and the two set off on the two hundred-mile journey. It was a decision that would bring Byron and Shelley together again, lead to the first of Shelley's great Italian works, but cost Shelley and Mary dear in terms of their own family.

It was at this point that perhaps the most notorious review in the English language made its appearance, Lockhart's review of Keats's 'Endymion' in *Blackwood's Magazine*. There had been, unluckily, a chance meeting between Lockhart and Keats's friend Benjamin Bailey in July, when Bailey had loyally tried to dissociate Keats from Hunt and his circle, but in doing so had given Lockhart a run-down on Keats's relatively humble background and his surgical apprenticeship. Suddenly realising that he might exploit this information to attack Keats, he asked him not to make use of it in any review, to which Lockhart replied that it would not be used by *him*. Of course, this left the anonymous 'Z' free to employ it as an additional line of attack.

Today it is taken for granted that success in the music business can lift people – by reason of their talent – from their situations to undreamed of lives. Elvis grew up on the wrong side of the tracks in Mississippi, Glenn Campbell came from a family of sharecroppers, Percy Sledge hit the big time when he released 'When a Man Loves a Woman' – the stories go on and on, with that of the Beatles being one of the most celebrated. Today, by and large, such examples are acclaimed in newspapers, magazines and accepted by their readerships. That's just taken as a given, with the press and the music business (generally) enjoying a mutually beneficial relationship.

This democratization of culture was, shall we say, 'in development' in the early 19th century. As is well known, Shakespeare was described as an 'upstart crow' because he was not of the class or educational background that was regarded as proper for a writer. That attitude, if Lockhart's review of Keats's 'Endymion' is anything to go on, was still going strong in 1818.

He began by arguing, with unashamed snobbery, that the 'mad age' they lived in was afflicted by the belief of 'farm servants, unmarried ladies … and footmen' that they could write poetry. 'It is with such sorrow as this that we have contemplated the case of Mr John Keats. This young man appears to have received from nature talents of an excellent, perhaps even of a superior order—talents which, devoted to the purposes of any useful profession, must have rendered him a respectable, if not an eminent citizen. His friends, we understand, destined him to the career of medicine and he was bound apprentice some years ago to a worthy apothecary in town. But all has been undone by a sudden attack of the malady to which we have alluded….'

After attacking him for allying himself with Hunt in his sonnet 'Written on the day that Mr Leigh Hunt left Prison', he then was utterly infuriated by Keats's 'Sonnet to

Haydon' which had proposed that 'Great spirits now on earth are sojourning' and had ended with the words: 'Hear ye not the hum/Of mighty workings? Listen ye nations, and be dumb!'

'The nations are to listen and be dumb! And why, good Johnny Keats? Because Leigh Hunt is editor of *The Examiner*, and Haydon has painted the judgment of Solomon, and you and Cornelius Webb, and a few more city sparks, are pleased to look upon yourselves as so many future Shakespeares and Miltons! The world has really some reason to look to its foundations!'

His association with Hunt and the 'Cockney School' also drew fire: 'We had almost forgot to mention, that Keats belongs to the Cockney School of Politics, as well as the Cockney School of Poetry. It is fit that he who holds Rimini to be the first poem, should believe *The Examiner* to be the first politician of the day. We admire consistency, even in folly... how their bantling has already learned to lisp sedition'.

Lockhart's parting shot showed him at his meanest: 'It is a better and a wiser thing to be a starved apothecary than a starved poet; so back to the shop Mr John, back to 'plasters, pills, and ointment boxes', &c. But, for Heaven's sake, young Sangrado, be a little more sparing of extenuatives and soporifics in your practice than you have been in your poetry'.

Walter Scott would later get some feedback on his son-in-law's invective. Southey 'commented to Scott in 1824 of that injustice and cruelty shown to Keats', a criticism that Scott seems to have taken to heart. For Keats's future carer in Rome Joseph Severn 'testified that... when he met Sir Walter Scott in Rome many years after, he was at a loss to understand Scott's embarrassment when Keats's name was mentioned; and it was not until a friend afterwards explained that Scott was connected with one of the magazines which was popularly supposed to have caused Keats's death that he could fathom it'.

Keats, back in London, reacted calmly to the abuse. 'My own domestic criticism has given me pain … beyond what Blackwood or the Quarterly could possibly inflict' he wrote to his publisher. As for 'Endymion', he wrote: 'In Endymion', I leaped headlong into the Sea, and thereby have become better acquainted with the Soundings, the quicksands, & the rocks, than if I had stayed upon the green shore, and piped a silly pipe, and took tea & comfortable advice.—I was never afraid of failure; for I would sooner fail than not be among the greatest'.

The Beatles, when faced with rejection in their early days had their confidence-building ritual: 'When the Beatles were depressed we had this little chant', John Lennon recalled. 'I would yell out, 'Where are we going, fellows?' They would say, 'To the top, Johnny,' in pseudo-American voices. And I would say, 'Where is that, fellows?' And they would say, 'To the toppermost of the poppermost'. It was some dumb expression from a cheap movie…'

They knew they had something to offer a monochrome and downbeat era; similarly Keats knew he could bring a new dimension to the poetry of the time. 'The lines of Pope's verse are like mice, compared to my own' he wrote, and shortly after Lockhart's scathing review he was writing to his brother 'I think I shall be among the English poets after my death'. There is also a tantalizing fragment when he told a friend 'Byron and Shelley think they are to lead the age, but....'

What has been described as his 'living year' had begun. As his introduction to 'Endymion' had concluded, 'I hope I have not in too late a day touched the beautiful mythology of Greece and dulled its brightness: for I wish to try once more, before I bid it farewell'.

Now he had embarked on 'Hyperion', with its classic opening:

> Deep in the shady sadness of a vale
> Far sunken from the healthy breath of morn,
> Far from the fiery noon, and eve's one star,
> Sat gray-hair'd Saturn, quiet as a stone,
> Still as the silence round about his lair;
> Forest on forest hung about his head
> Like cloud on cloud. No stir of air was there,
> Not so much life as on a summer's day
> Robs not one light seed from the feather'd grass,
> But where the dead leaf fell, there did it rest. ....

The story was that of the Titans, including Saturn, Oceanus, and Hyperion, being displaced and overthrown by the Olympians – including Jupiter, Neptune and Apollo. So it was a tale of political change, with the Titans reluctant to accept their fate, and Hyperion in particular incandescent with rage, sorrow and defiance:

> He enter'd, but he enter'd full of wrath;
> His flaming robes stream'd out beyond his heels,
> And gave a roar, as if of earthly fire,
> That scar'd away the meek ethereal Hours

And made their dove-wings tremble. On he flared,
From stately nave to nave, from vault to vault…

… Saturn is fallen, am I too to fall?
Am I to leave this haven of my rest,
This cradle of my glory, this soft clime,
This calm luxuriance of blissful light,
These crystalline pavilions, and pure fanes,
Of all my lucent empire?

However, when the fallen Titans gather, Oceanus, who has accepted that Neptune is worthy of replacing him, speaks up, and says, in effect, 'Let It Be' – a phrase entering the poem itself:

…on our heels a fresh perfection treads,
A power more strong in beauty, born of us
And fated to excel us …

… shall the tree be envious of the dove
Because it cooeth, and hath snowy wings
To wander wherewithal and find its joys?
We are such forest-trees, and our fair boughs
Have bred forth, not pale solitary doves,
But eagles golden-feather'd, who do tower
Above us in their beauty, and must reign
In right thereof; for 'tis the eternal law
That first in beauty should be first in might…

Receive the truth, and let it be your balm'.

Among all the travails of 19th century Britain, with its deprived and unrepresented working classes, Keats was, perhaps, commenting indirectly on the contemporary situation, addressing the ruling oligarchy in Britain when he wrote of 'the fresh perfection' that 'is fated to excel us'.

For those working classes were awakening and the landowning elite were losing their economic supremacy as the industrial revolution gathered pace. Maybe Keats was reading himself into the situation of the old oligarchy, and offering up a kind of oblique Shakespearean advice. In the end its story is of impending change, so Keats, by design or not, is preparing the reader, and the nation at large, for that change. It can be seen as an unconscious strategy that would recur a year later, when he wrote what may have been his final poem 'To Autumn'.

By September Byron was well settled into the Palazzo Mocenigo. A month earlier he had written to his half-sister Augusta Leigh that 'My little girl, Allegra ... has been with me these three months: she is very pretty, remarkably intelligent, and a great favourite with everybody'. But soon after, what with quarrelling servants and assorted flamboyant mistresses (who also quarrelled), he had sent her to the Hoppners, the development which had so troubled Claire in Bagni di Lucca and led to her, and Shelley, journeying to Venice.

So one late September afternoon Shelley called at the palazzo, writing to Mary that Byron 'was delighted to see me; & our first conversation of course consisted in the object of my visit....' Though unwilling to hand Allegra over to Claire on a permanent basis, he did offer to lend

Shelley and his household his leased villa in Este as a space where mother and child could reunite.

He then, Shelley continued, 'took me in his gondola … across the laguna to a long sandy island which defends Venice from the Adriatic. When we disembarked, we found his horses waiting, & rode along the sands of the sea talking'.

Paul McCartney has often spoken of how he would tell acquaintances in Liverpool how he would write songs and always got a noncommittal response – until he met John Lennon: 'So do I!' came the reply. The mutual inspiration and competition that resulted from their subsequent partnership would be the underlying drive behind the Beatles.

There was a similar process of inspiration mingled with competition in Byron and Shelley's case. Almost immediately Shelley's poetic drought came to an end, as he embarked on 'Julian and Maddalo', drawing on their conversations, describing his and Byron's intellectual interplay:

> I rode one evening with Count Maddalo
> Upon the bank of land which breaks the flow
> Of Adria towards Venice: a bare strand
> Of hillocks, heap'd from ever-shifting sand,
> Matted with thistles and amphibious weeds…
>
> So, as we rode, we talked …
> …Of all that earth has been or yet may be,
> All that vain men imagine or believe,
> Or hope can paint or suffering may achieve,

> We descanted, and I (for ever still
> Is it not wise to make the best of ill?)
> Argu'd against despondency, but pride
> Made my companion take the darker side…

So the poem outlines the conflict between the optimistic outlook of Julian, the Shelley persona:

> We know
> That we have power over ourselves to do
> And suffer—what, we know not till we try;
> But something nobler than to live and die:
> So taught those kings of old philosophy
> Who reign'd, before Religion made men blind;
> And those who suffer with their suffering kind
> Yet feel their faith, religion

and the scepticism of Maddalo, the character based on Byron:

> "My dear friend,"
> Said Maddalo, "my judgement will not bend
> To your opinion, though I think you might
> Make such a system refutation-tight
> As far as words go".

Praised for its self-awareness and psychological insight, 'Julian and Maddalo' reveals the fertilities and frictions in the Shelley-Byron relationship. They stimulated each other, undoubtedly, with Shelley energised by Byron's position as a poet with all the power of a popular audience, and Byron delighting in interrogating Shelley's pantheistic, utopian metaphysics but accepting his overall poetic knowledge and sincerity.

Indeed, Julian contemplates staying on in Venice, where:

> I might sit,
> In Maddalo's great palace, and his wit
> And subtle talk would cheer the winter night
> And make me know myself.

After leaving Venice and setting off towards Naples Shelley wrote to Peacock informing him that a new Byron poem was making its appearance. 'He read me the first canto of Don Juan, a thing in the style of Beppo, but infinitely better....' But he was troubled by Byron's lifestyle. After moving to Naples in December he told Peacock that not only did his gondolieri pick up people from the street for him, but 'he allows mothers and daughters to bargain with him for their daughters, and though this is common enough in Italy, yet for an Englishman to encourage such sickening vice is a melancholy thing...'

Afterwards he added, in a clear indication of how Allegra's situation was a source of tension between himself and Byron: 'You may think how unwillingly *I* have left my little favourite (Allegra *cancelled*) Alba in a situation where she might fall again under his authority. But I have employed arguments entreaties everything in vain, & when these fail you know I no longer have any right'. He even half-hoped that Allegra would return to them after Byron had come to a violent end: 'for his sake I ought to hope that his career must end up soon by some violent circumstance which must reduce our situation with respect to Alba into its antient tie'.

A few days later however, writing to Hunt, his tone was more moderate. Though 'Our poor friend Lord Byron is quite corrupted by living among these people; and in fact is going on in a way not very worthy of him' he noted that Hunt was definitely in Byron's thoughts. 'He talked a great deal about you, and among other things he said that he wished you could come to Italy and bade me tell you that he would lend you money for the journey (4 or £500)… Write to me quickly what you think of this plan on which my imagination delights itself….'

Getting Leigh Hunt, his 'best and only friend', to Italy had been on Shelley's mind ever since leaving England. Now Lord Byron, despite the tensions over Allegra, was becoming a potential factor in the realization of Shelley's hopes. A triangular dynamic now drove Shelley's relationship with Byron: his admiration for Byron's poetic gifts, the ever-worrisome issue of Allegra, and his dependence on Byron's offices to bring Hunt to Italy.

Back in England, Hunt would eventually reply 'I cannot come; I wish to God that I would; but it is next to impossible' As a working writer 'it is more than ever necessary that I should be every Saturday at office'. In fact when Shelley wrote he was producing a new edition of his 'Literary Pocket Book', 'handy little volumes of poetry and prose', also containing information on 'what's on and where' for the literary traveller. Priced at half a crown, they were a financial success, though they did not please Keats.

In a letter to George and Georgiana, making their way to Louisville, Kentucky, he wrote 'Hunt keeps on in his old way – I am completely tired of it all. He has lately published a Pocket Book called the literary Pocket Book – full of the most sickening stuff you can imagine'.

This was despite the fact that Hunt had included two Keats sonnets in the collection, and had presented a copy to him. Possibly Charles Brown, who both had a caustic tongue and often looked askance at Keats's friends and acquaintances, had influenced some of Keats's comments at this time. He continued with even more withering remarks: though Hunt was 'certainly a pleasant fellow in the main when you are with him … in reality he is vain, egotistical and disgusting in matters of taste and in morals'. He 'does one harm by making fine things petty and beautiful things hateful. … This distorts one's mind – makes one's thoughts bizarre – perplexes one in the standard of beauty'.

However, though an irritant, Hunt was obviously still a factor in Keats's life. He was there for Keats for comfort and sympathy after his brother Tom had died on 1st December, also offering to introduce him to Byron's friend Tom Moore. His work on *The Examiner* still influenced the young poet: in the same letter Keats noted 'There is a letter today in *The Examiner* to the Electors of Westminster on Mr Hobhouse's account. In it there is a good account of Cobbett – I have not the paper by me or I would copy it'.

The year of 1818 would come to an end, then, with Hunt very much alive in the minds of Keats, Shelley and Byron. The three poets were in their creative prime; Keats had made good progress with 'Hyperion', also completing some shorter poems, Shelley had completed the first Act of 'Prometheus Unbound' while Byron had finished the first canto of 'Don Juan' and was working on the second. As he would come to write, in lines that would apply to all three poets and their historic achievements:

> But words are things, and a small drop of ink,
> Falling like dew, upon a thought, produces
> That which makes thousands, perhaps millions, think.

9

The 'Sergeant Pepper Year'

The year 1967 is universally held to be a peak of Beatles creativity. Their first full year without touring, they released what is sometimes called the best pop single ever, 'Strawberry Fields Forever' with 'Penny Lane', continued pioneering the format of the music video at the same time, recorded and released 'Sergeant Pepper', participated in the first global live broadcast with 'All You Need Is Love', then produced the film and soundtrack 'Magical Mystery Tour'. Oh yes, and they finished by throwing off a final No. 1 single 'Hello, Goodbye' backed with 'I Am The Walrus'.

1819 is also held to be a peak year of Romantics creativity. All of John Keats's greatest works were written in that year: 'Lamia', 'The Eve of St. Agnes', the great odes ('On Indolence', 'On a Grecian Urn', 'To Psyche', 'To a Nightingale', 'On Melancholy', and 'To Autumn'), and the two versions of 'Hyperion'.

For Shelley too it was a year often called his Annus Mirabilis. It started in Naples, where he worked on 'Julian and Maddalo', continued in Rome where he added two Acts to 'Prometheus Unbound', then, following the death of his son William, carried on in Livorno where wrote his play 'The Cenci' and then one of his most powerful and still resonant poems, 'The Mask of Anarchy'. In Florence he then wrote the 'Ode to the West Wind' and 'Peter Bell the Third', and still pondering the issues raised by the Peterloo

Massacre, began work on his essay 'A Philosophical View of Reform'. He also completed a fourth Act of 'Prometheus Unbound', sending a fair copy to his London publishers at the end of the year.

Byron began the year with two cantos of 'Don Juan' completed, and had sent the first to his friends in London for an opinion. He had been eager for their view of it, having noted to his friend Tom Moore that 'it is meant to be a little quietly facetious on everything … but I doubt whether it is not … too free for these modest days'. Its opening lines –

> I want a hero: an uncommon want,
> When every year and month sends forth a new one,
> Till, after cloying the gazettes with cant,
> The age discovers he is not the true one…

established its tone perfectly: the view from home, however, was that despite its wit, liveliness and poetry it was unpublishable. With its dedication squarely aimed at poet laureate Robert Southey – 'an epic renegade' – and its inclusion of a bawdy reference – 'And fall for lack of moisture quite a dry Bob', a piece of Regency slang for 'coition without male emission' – they concluded that 'you could not publish it unless you were over here ready to fight him'.

On reflection, however, as the new year began, Byron decided to defy what he called the 'puritanical committee'. 'If they had said the poetry was bad, I would have acquiesced; but they say the contrary, and then talk to me about morality… I maintain that it is the most moral of poems, but if people won't discover the moral, that is their fault, not mine'. And he faced down Murray's desire to cut some of the 'indelicacies' – 'You won't make Canticles of my cantos … I won't have any of your damned cutting and slashing'. And so, in July, the first two cantos were published – though anonymously, and on Byron's direction without the dedication attacking Southey.

His life in Venice may have sounded spectacular in terms of his love life, but the string of mindless liaisons were beginning to pall. In April they came to an end, when he met, one evening, a young lady of nineteen, Contessa Teresa Guiccioli. Unhappily married to a 58-year-old Count from Ravenna, Byron described her as being 'as fair as sunrise, and warm as noon' and also, with her glaringly unsuitable marriage, 'sacrificed to wealth, filial duty and all that'. That evening, after being introduced to this 'peer of England and its greatest poet', she held Byron in a way that his succession of mistresses could not, with her talk of Dante, Petrarch and Boccaccio. That month he wrote to her 'You who are my only and last love, who are my only joy', and two months later he dedicated a new poem, 'The Prophecy of Dante', to her. There was none of his frequent masking of his feelings in the work – it was a passionately sincere paean to Italian independence, a call to action, spoken as if by the great Italian bard from his exile in Ravenna – and possibly the closest to Shelley that he ever came.

The early months of 1819 had seen Keats in an unsettled and depressed state of mind, not only full of sorrow over Tom's death but occasionally succumbing to morbid thoughts about his lack of progress. The all-conquering Byron was still irking him. 'He describes what he sees – I describe what I imagine. Mine is the harder task' he said in February, and 'he commented gloomily on Byron's sale of 4,000 copies of the last canto of Childe Harold'. In addition, 'he was touchy of anything like a joke on his status as a poet. 'When kind Mr Lewis said to gossiping Mrs Brawne 'He is quite the little poet' Keats burst out 'You see what it is to be under six feet and not a Lord'.

Then, in April, he added a waspish comment to a piece of literary gossip, perhaps relayed by Hunt, regarding a forthcoming parody of a new Wordsworth poem. 'A few days ago Hunt dined here .... Wordsworth is going to publish a poem called Peter Bell .... Reynolds hearing that ... took it into his head to write a skit upon it called Peter Bell – it comes out before the real Peter Bell... It would be just as well to trounce Lord Byron in the same manner'.

He tried to go deeper into Byron's nature in another letter. 'A man's life of any worth is a continual allegory – and very few eyes can see the mystery of life – a life like the Scriptures, figurative... Lord Byron cuts a figure, but he is not figurative. Shakespeare led a life of allegory: his works are the comments on it'.

The great poems that would make up his final volume of poetry – which 'would come to be recognised as one of the most important poetic works ever published', were stacking up. Like the George Harrison of 'Something' and 'Here Comes the Sun', he was more than equalling his two illustrious contemporaries. On a visit to Chichester in February, drawing on its historic ambience, he had written the 'Eve of St Agnes', with its perfect introductory stanza, its gorgeous sensuality as the story unfolds, and its climactic conclusion as the lovers triumph and flee into the night.

Keats had given the English language one of its great narratives of youthful love; in April he added 'La Belle Dame sans Merci', and in May those four great Odes, 'On Melancholy', 'To Psyche', 'On Indolence', and 'To a Grecian Urn'. There would be more to come in the final part of the year.

At this point it would be over two years before Shelley and Byron would meet again, but they were both still very much aware of each other. A lurid account of the famous 'Frankenstein' summer had been published in a London magazine, and Byron, who to the end of his days would defend Shelley and his character, wrote to Murray in May, denying the article's allegations of incest (which he thought had come from Robert Southey), and pointing to the great achievement of the time, Mary's 'Frankenstein'.

'The story of the agreement to write the Ghost-books is true … Mary Godwin (now Mrs Shelley) wrote *Frankenstein* … Methinks it is a wonderful work for a girl of nineteen, - *not* nineteen, indeed, at the time'.

After a difficult, still not understood residence in Naples, Shelley's spirits had lifted when they moved to Rome that March. The Forum, the Colosseum and the Baths of Caracalla became his favourite haunts, with the latter becoming his outdoor study where his work on 'Prometheus Unbound' continued. After 'Queen Mab' and 'The Revolt of Islam', it was his third epic poem championing human freedom, a work described by W.B. Yeats as 'among the sacred books of the world'.

'Prometheus Unbound' can be seen as a high culture version of the fourth of the Beatles films, the animated psychedelic fantasy 'Yellow Submarine'. The plots are essentially the same, with similar tyrannies (for Jupiter read the Blue Meanies) being overthrown by the forces of life. In Shelley's play Prometheus is chained to a rock by Jupiter for the crime of bringing fire to humanity; in 'Yellow Submarine' Pepperland is enslaved by the music-hating Blue Meanies. In the end both tyrannies are overthrown by the power of Love, with the pronouncement by Prometheus that he forgives Jupiter being the key to his downfall. In their turn the Blue Meanies and their various allies, even the fearsome Flying Glove, are overcome by 'All You Need is Love'. 'Prometheus Unbound' ends with a vision of a reimagined and transformed world, with a new age dawning on earth. And should the old order return, Shelley ends the poem by citing the ways 'by which to reassume, An empire o'er the disentangled doom'.

For its part 'Yellow Submarine' ends with a similar reworking of reality, with the final song, 'It's All Too Much', evoking a transformative Love shining all around. The transformation extends to the real world, with John Lennon inviting the vanquished Meanies to join them, 'hook up and otherwise commingle'. So the film ends on a reconciliatory note, with the triumph of nonviolence and of good over evil: 'This is what sets the film in such a sacred space' comments the blogger Erich Kuersten, providing a contemporary counterpoint to Yeats's commentary on Shelley's poem.

Putting 'Prometheus Unbound' alongside 'Yellow Submarine' reveals shows how society has changed in the years between the Younger Romantics and The Beatles. 'Prometheus Unbound' was cast in a form that would, Shelley thought, appeal to well-educated *Examiner* readers – 'the more select classes of poetical readers' – as he put it in his introduction to the poem. Well-versed in the classics as they were likely to be, they would instantly see how he was updating 'Prometheus Bound' from Aeschylus and understand its contemporary relevance to the politics of the day.

That world of ancient Greece, in which Shelley and Byron (and to a lesser extent Keats) were steeped, has largely receded from the popular imagination, succeeded by a world of mass entertainment in which 'Yellow Submarine' landed perfectly. Despite their differing cultural hinterlands, Shelley's mythic drama and the Beatles' film are of the same mind, singing the same song, one could say, across the centuries.

Their stay in Rome saw Shelley and Mary hit by another personal tragedy: on the 7th June their last surviving child William died of malaria. He was buried in the Protestant cemetery; on the 10th the Shelleys, now childless, left the city and headed for Livorno, where the Gisbornes helped them secure a three month lease on a house on the outskirts of Livorno. It was topped with an upper room where Shelley set up his study; he could look out over the fields to the sea, a view varied and enlivened by dramatic storms which broke over the landscape.

Keats was in Shelley's thoughts; having requested a copy of 'Endymion' from his publisher Charles Ollier a year previously he now reports back – in a letter dated September 6th 1819 – that he has read it. But, like many a reader, he has found it tough going:

'For the 2nd in this list (Endymion) much praise is due to me for having read, The Author's intention appearing to be that no person should possibly get to the end of it. Yet it is full of the highest & the finest gleams of poetry; I think if he had printed about 50 pages of fragments from it I should have been led to admire Keats as a poet more than I ought, of which now there is no danger'.

The same letter contained a request that copies of any new publications be sent to Keats, and also his first mention of the dramatic and tragic events in Manchester: 'The same day that your letter came, came the news of the Manchester work, & the torrent of my indignation has not yet done boiling in my veins. I wait anxiously to hear how the Country will express its sense of this bloody murderous oppression of its destroyers….'

The event that Shelley referred to would become known as the Peterloo Massacre. When a peaceable crowd of 60,000 people had gathered in Manchester to demonstrate for parliamentary reform, the meeting had been disrupted by militia and cavalry; there had been around a dozen deaths and around 600 people had been wounded.

It created a sense of political crisis in the country, with the government introducing repressive legislation and suspending Habeas Corpus, fears of political revolution on the French model from their side and warnings about the need for reform from the other.

All very like 1968, with the Vietnam War and the Tet Offensive dividing the politics of the day, and the youth movement in Europe and the USA becoming increasingly politicised. The atmosphere of social upheaval and the calls for violent revolution from the New Left led John Lennon to think that the Beatles should contribute to the debate. 'I thought it was about time we spoke about it, the same as I thought it was about time we stopped not answering about the Vietnamese war [in 1966]. I had been thinking about it up in the hills in India'. Like Shelley back in the second decade of the 19th century, he would wrestle with the issue of violence, nonviolence and social change in his song 'Revolution'.

The first version of 'Revolution', in its slow doo-wop format, had a chorus that equivocated about participating in 'destruction', while the second was clear – 'you can count me out'. Similarly, Shelley seemed to be riding two horses in 'The Mask of Anarchy', his immediate response to Peterloo. His ringing words –

> Rise like Lions after slumber
> In unvanquishable number–
> Shake your chains to earth like dew
> Which in sleep had fallen on you–
> Ye are many – they are few

sound like a call for violent revolution, but they were offset by the major part of the work, from stanza 39 onwards, that make it clear that the revolution he envisages is nonviolent in nature. They were lines that would echo in history, influencing Gandhi during his campaign for Indian Independence and afterwards working through to Martin Luther King and the Civil Rights Movement in 1960s America. For the Cameroonian scholar, George Ewane Dgidi, 'Percy Bysshe Shelley is the unrivalled father of nonviolence as an ethical and pragmatic philosophy'.

However, Shelley would find the issue he was tackling, whether violence is ever justified as a way of resisting oppression, was too complicated to be satisfactorily explored through verse. So he followed his poetic fireworks with his essay 'A Philosophical View of Reform', in which he concludes that as a last resort, if all peaceful methods have been tried, the people have what he called 'the last resort of resistance', that of insurrection. And, he continued, 'The right of insurrection is derived from the employment of armed force to counteract the will of the nation'.

So he was looking for a democratic mandate, and 'though the true friend of mankind and his country would hesitate before he recommended measures which tend to bring down so heavy a calamity as war' there could be times when 'the madness of parties admits no other mode of determining the question at issue'.

Which is why, perhaps, Lennon's lines 'But when you talk about destruction, Don't you know you can count me out (and in)' – still have their place. As he would acknowledge later: when pressed about the use of force to resist Nazism in the Second World War, he replied 'What happened then was right for the time'.

At this point John Keats was in Winchester, where the air 'was worth sixpence a pint', lodging in a quiet street near the Cathedral, with money worries assuaged by a recent payment from his publishers, and with his poem 'Lamia' completed. He had the space to work, and felt himself to be in a 'state for the best sort of poetry'.

He launched into a reworking of 'Hyperion', influenced by Dante's 'Inferno', where Dante had been guided through the underworld by Virgil. Using a similar scheme, Keats would be guided by Moneta, Goddess of Knowledge, who would show him the world of the fallen Titans and lead him to a deeper understanding of his poetic vocation. For five days he wrote, but an interruption, in the form of a desperate letter from his brother George, caused him to break off and take the night coach to London. George had run into financial difficulties in America, and needed help.

It was during this visit to London that John Keats would have his second Aunt Mimi-style put-down from his guardian Richard Abbey. In John Lennon's case it came on December 8th 1960, exactly 20 years before his death. Mimi had already issued her famous warning about guitars and financial instability – now, that December night, her counsel seemed all too accurate.

The Beatles had returned from Hamburg in disarray: George had been deported for working underage, Paul and Pete Best had also been deported after a fire had broken out in their quarters, and John Lennon had returned by train and now was regretting his early assurance to Mimi about his future financial prospects. 'Where's your £100 a week now John?' she shouted at him as he woke her up and asked her to pay the taxi fare.

In Keats's case it was several years since Abbey had been appalled at his abandonment of his medical career – 'John, you are either mad or a Fool, to talk in so absurd a Manner'. Now they were meeting up again, after the first two volumes of Keats's poems had made little impression critically or financially. His previous counsel also seemed all too accurate, and like Aunt Mimi, he could not help commenting on the young poet's lack of success, reactivating Keats's resentment of Byron in the process. As Keats wrote to his brother George:

'He began blowing up Lord Byron while I was sitting with him: 'However, maybe the fellow says some true things now and then', at which he took up a magazine, and read me some extracts from Don Juan (Lord Byron's last flash poem), and particularly one against literary ambition'. Rubbing Keats's nose in the critical and financial failure of his work he quoted Byron on the foolishness of the quest for literary fame:

Some liken it to climbing up a hill,
Whose summit, like all hills, is lost in vapour

As will be seen, in John Keats's case the hard-headed advice of the realist, in worldly, or strictly financial terms at least, proved to be right. It would only be years after his death that an audience caught up with his work. In John Lennon's case there was a happier denouement. According to his own account he spent three weeks in virtual solitude, wondering whether to continue with the band. He remembered later 'I was so fed up I didn't bother to contact the others for a few weeks. A month is a long time at eighteen or nineteen; I didn't know what they were doing. I just withdrew to think whether it was worth going on with'.

The act of faith that went into his re-emergence was touched with hard-headedness, as he recalled: 'Anyway, after a while I got to thinking that we ought to cash in on the Liverpool beat scene. Things were really thriving and it seemed a pity to waste the experience we'd got, playing all those hours every night in Hamburg'. He was right about that; the Beatles historian Mark Lewisohn has estimated that The Beatles spent a total of 957 hours playing on stage in Hamburg, and the difference it had made was immediately apparent. After a gig at the Litherland Town Hall, where the audience was amazed at the transformation that had taken place, they then got regular spots at the Cavern, where, in time, Brian Epstein would turn up to see them. This time the audience was ready and waiting.

Despite the irritation that went with his encounter with Abbey, Keats's visit to London gave him a vital insight into the post-Peterloo atmosphere. While he was making his way along Fleet Street to meet with him he had been caught up in a mass demonstration of 30,000 Londoners welcoming Henry Hunt, the main speaker at Peterloo, to the city. 'The whole distance from the Angel at Islington to the Crown and Anchor was lined with multitudes' Keats reported to his brother. Hunt's entourage included a young man bearing sabre wounds from the day. It was a vivid reminder of the ongoing political impasse, that seemed to threaten social and financial meltdown.

So Keats had much to reflect on when he returned to Winchester. And yet, when a poetic response came, in the form of his ode 'To Autumn', it seemed to have very little to do with the situation facing the country at large.

'How beautiful the season is now – a temperate sharpness in the air' Keats wrote a few days after its completion. 'Somehow a stubble plain looks warm – this struck me so much on my Sunday's walk that I composed upon it'.

While 'To Autumn' can simply be seen as a nature poem celebrating the countryside around Winchester, modern readings tend to stress that the Peterloo massacre is in the background as an influence. Some argue that the bees in the poem refer to the downtrodden workers in Manchester, but perhaps the crisis over Peterloo emerges in its sense of focus and concentration. There is also the insinuation that just as that tranquil scene would be transformed by the approaching winter, so change would come to the current political stalemate.

So maybe on some level Keats – who once wrote that he 'hoped to add something to the liberal side of the question', *was* writing about change: political change would come just as seasonal change would inevitably follow that tranquil late summer evening. But that is there for you and your imagination, given freedom by the quality of 'indistinctness', which some describe as one of the greatest artistic qualities. It can be seen as being at the heart of Paul McCartney songs like 'Hey Jude', 'The Long and Winding Road', or 'Yesterday'; as he put it recently: 'I like my songs to be for everyman, or everywoman … I like the fact that they put their own interpretations on them … because it's yours now, I've let go so now you should make of it what you want'.

But there's also a case for the directness of John Lennon's songs: as he once told David Bowie, 'It's very easy – all you have to do is say what you mean, make it rhyme and put a backbeat to it'. This crucial distinction between the two was mirrored by Keats and Shelley's contrasting approaches, certainly in their immediate responses to Peterloo.

Having dismissed 'Don Juan' as a 'flash poem' in his letter to George, Keats now, resuming 'The Fall of Hyperion' from his Winchester lodgings, put a critique of Byron into the work, including him in the category of

all mock lyrists, large self worshipers,
And careless Hectorers in proud bad verse.

He had come a long, long way from his early admiration for Byron, and his description of 'Childe Harold's Pilgrimage' as 'a tale of pleasing woe'.

If Peterloo formed part of the background to 'To Autumn', it also critically influenced Shelley's 'Ode to the West Wind', written about two months after the 'Mask of Anarchy'. Though there is no mention of the poem in his or Mary's letters, he clearly believed it to be a key work, for he referred to it 18 months later, on the final stanza of 'Adonais':

That breath whose might I have invoked in song,
Descends on me….

That breath was the 'wild West wind' that blew through the trees in the forest of the Cascina in Florence in October 1819, and after Peterloo, his inability to influence the situation through his work, the death of William and a savage attack on his life and work in the *Quarterly Review*, it was a poem that re-activated Shelley's creativity and sense of poetic direction.

The 'Ode to the West Wind' shares this quality of artistic and personal renewal with a key work by John Lennon, 'Strawberry Fields Forever' – which Lennon also referred back to, in the opening line of the White Album's 'Glass Onion'.

Like Shelley in Florence, Lennon found himself in a state of limbo, in his case due to the end of The Beatles' touring career which, from the beginning, had been a central part of their existence. Where were they to go from here?

What he did in Almeria in Spain, where he wrote 'Strawberry Fields Forever', was to reach back to that carefree and untroubled time in his boyhood when he and his friends went to garden parties at the Strawberry Fields Salvation Army orphanage near his home. 'We'd all go up there and hang out and sell lemonade bottles for a penny and we always had fun at Strawberry Fields' he recalled later.

'Strawberry Fields Forever' then, evokes that boyhood experience, where he would climb a tree and wonder about the nature of his being and his sense of distinctiveness. Perhaps its lyrics are a perfect example of the state that Keats had described as that of 'Negative Capability': the 'quality (that) went to form a Man of

Achievement especially in Literature & which Shakespeare possessed so enormously—I mean *Negative Capability*, that is when man is capable of being in uncertainties, Mysteries, doubts, without any irritable reaching after fact & reason'. In any case, that was the boyhood experience that he drew on and projected into the future – 'Strawberry Fields Forever'!

The 'Ode to the West Wind' also looks back to boyhood, when it seemed, that in his youthful omnipotence, he could outrun the wind itself:

If even
I were as in my boyhood, and could be
The comrade of thy wanderings over heaven;
As then, when to outstrip thy skiey speed
Scarce seemed a vision…

So like Lennon he centres himself with that thought of youthful freedom. And just as 'Strawberry Fields' would find a direction for the Beatles and lead on to 'Sergeant Pepper', so Shelley's 'Ode to the West Wind' restored his confidence and ushered in the final phase of his writing career.

Be thou, Spirit fierce,
My spirit! Be thou me, impetuous one!

Drive my dead thoughts over the universe
Like withered leaves to quicken a new birth!

And, by the incantation of this verse,
Scatter, as from an unextinguished hearth
Ashes and sparks, my words among mankind!

Be through my lips to unawakened Earth
The trumpet of a prophecy! O Wind,
If Winter comes, can Spring be far behind?

So the year of 1819 came to an end with Shelley still on fire in creative terms, adding that fourth, final, utopian Act to 'Prometheus Unbound', completing his satire on Wordsworth 'Peter Bell the Third', and still working on his essay 'A Philosophical View of Reform'. In publication terms though he was often stymied. Corresponding with Hunt at regular intervals, he enquired after 'Julian and Maddalo' which he hoped could be printed in *The Examiner*, but Hunt did not respond. Neither had he acknowledged 'The Mask of Anarchy', which Shelley had sent him, nor 'Peter Bell The Third'.

Hunt, as ever busy with *The Examiner*, and now with an additional publication *The Indicator* to produce, thought he could not risk publishing 'The Mask of Anarchy'. It would almost certainly have landed him with another lengthy jail term. He did, however, publish it after the passage of the Great Reform Bill in 1832, when the post-Peterloo political crisis had subsided.

John Keats was back in London, still lodging in his friend Charles Brown's house, Wentworth Place, in Hampstead, in love with Fanny Brawne in an adjoining apartment and now engaged to her. He professed himself bored with London society; confiding to his sister-in-law in the U.S.A. that 'If I go to Hunt's, I run my head into many tunes heard before, old puns and old music… At Dilke's I fall foul of politics. …. 'Tis best to remain aloof from people and like their good parts without being eternally troubled with the dull process of their every-day lives. … All I can say is that, standing at Charing Cross and looking east, west, north and south I see nothing but dullness'.

He was in touch with his publisher John Taylor about a new edition of poems but saw his attempts to write plays for Covent Garden as a better career path. Sadly, the plays he worked on with Brown – 'Otho the Great', 'King Stephen' and 'The Cap and Bells' – did not succeed in commercial terms and have never been seen as his best work. 'The Cap and Bells' however, showed that Byron was still influencing him: he quoted from his last poem from England:

He bow'd at Bellanaine, and said—'Poor Bell!
Farewell! farewell! and if for ever! still
For ever fare thee well!'—and then he fell
A laughing!—snapp'd his fingers!—shame it is to tell!

Lord Byron himself was now far indeed from his old life on England. He had moved to Ravenna, and was living, somewhat bizarrely, in the upstairs apartment of Teresa's husband's palace. He was now her acknowledged 'Cavaliere Servente'; as he wrote back to friends in London 'I now confine myself to the strictest adultery'. In addition he was being drawn into the emerging struggle for Italian independence, storing arms for the Carbonari, the secret society whose dreams would come to fruition about 40 years later.

10

'There's a shadow hanging over me'

You could say Ringo Starr was fortunate. Thanks to medical advances over the past hundred years, and the availability of medical care that had developed in Britain he was able to recover, in the Myrtle Street Children's hospital in Liverpool, from the peritonitis that had followed an appendicitis operation. Admitted at the age of six, he was discharged two years later and though badly behind with reading and writing, was tutored by a neighbour who helped him catch up with his peer group. By the time he caught tuberculosis in 1953 the National Health Service had been established, and the national investment in health care that it represented paid off two years later, when he was again discharged fully recovered, though again badly behind at school.

The endless days in hospital had stimulated an interest that had been initiated and encouraged by hospital staff. 'I was in the hospital band' he recalled. 'That's where I really started playing. I never wanted anything else from there on ... My grandparents gave me a mandolin and a banjo, but I didn't want them. My grandfather gave me a harmonica ... we had a piano – nothing. Only the drums'.

Ringo's subsequent career demonstrates the truth of a statement by the World Bank: 'Investing in people through nutrition, health care, quality education, jobs and skills helps develop human capital, and this is key to ending extreme poverty and creating more inclusive societies'. Though unable to attend grammar school, unlike John, Paul and George, he would make a crucial contribution to the band he joined in 1962. As Jonathan Gould puts it 'Can't Buy Me Love', Ringo is always tagged as the lucky one for joining the Beatles but it was also a stroke of luck for them. Not only did he add a poetic touch to their names but at the very point that they were leaving Liverpool 'Ringo's presence ensured that, however far they ventured, they would always carry with them an unmistakable piece of home'.

In John Keats's time the germ theory of disease, which had led to the advances that had saved Ringo's life, was far from understood. So when he realised that he had contracted tuberculosis in 1819 he knew it was, almost undoubtedly, a death sentence. The story is famous. When, after returning from a trip to central London, on a bitterly cold February night with a biting wind, and travelling on the outside of the coach to save money, he arrived back home and went to bed, he coughed softly into a handkerchief. 'There is blood from my mouth' he said – 'bring me the candle, Brown, let me see this blood'. Looking at it with his doctor's eyes, knowing the difference between the oxygenated blood from the arteries and the blood that returns to the heart through the veins, he said calmly, 'I know the colour of that blood, it is arterial blood. I cannot be deceived in that colour. That drop of blood is my death warrant: I must die'.

Later in the year Keats and Hunt were to be brought closer together. As Brown always let Wentworth Place for the summer Keats would need alternative accommodation and care: Hunt, then living in Mortimer Terrace in Kentish Town, found him lodgings in Wesleyan Place, just round the corner from his own home. Then working on both *The Examiner* and *The Indicator*, he promptly published Keats's 'La Belle Dame Sans Merci' in the latter publication, as well as dedicating his translation of Tasso's play 'Aminta' to him.

John Taylor was hoping to issue a volume that would include 'Lamia', 'Isabella; or, The Pot of Basil', 'Hyperion', 'To Autumn', the four great Odes written a year previously, and other poems. Lonely in his new lodgings and without visits from Fanny Brawne to cheer him, Keats nevertheless continued work on his poems, correcting proofs in June. On the 22nd though, while starting off to town on a matter connected with his sister, his mouth again filled with blood, and he turned back, making for Hunt's place in Mortimer Terrace. There he encountered Maria Gisborne, the Shelleys' friend from Italy; it was through the Gisbornes that Shelley would hear of Keats's illness.

'We called in ... at Mr Hunt's house' – Maria Gisborne wrote in her diary – and were grieved to hear ... that Mr Keats was also ill in the house; he had burst a blood vessel the very night after we had seen him, and in order to be well attended, he had been removed from his lodgings in the neighbourhood, to Mr Hunt's house'.

Thus Hunt became Keats's primary carer. It was not easy with Hunt's notoriously uncontrolled and noisy family, and in addition the summer heat built as the days went by. Keats (almost certainly) contributed two passages to an essay in *The Indicator* published at the end of June, the first of which contained a memory of his sister at his grandmother's in Edmonton: 'Now the little girl at her grandmother's cottage door watches the coaches that go by, with her hand held up over her sunny forehead'. The other summed up his current situation: 'Now rooms with sun upon them become unbearable; and the apothecary's apprentice, with a bitterness beyond aloes, thinks of the pond he used to bathe in at school'.

Though the exact date that Keats's poems appeared is not known, at the end of June Taylor wrote to his father 'Next week Keats's new volume will be published, and if it does not sell well, I think nothing will ever sell again'.

Two weeks later Keats was writing: 'My book has had a good success among the literary people, and I believe, has had a moderate sale'. On the whole critics did not want to praise him unreservedly, but they would all pick a favourite, with 'To Autumn'. and 'Ode to a Nightingale' singled out for praise, and one reviewer anticipating posterity's judgement precisely: 'These poems are very far superior to any which their author has previously committed to the press. There is nothing showy, or extravagant, or eccentric about them; but they are pieces of calm beauty, or of lone and self-supported grandeur'. In addition, 'we do not think anything exceeds in silent grandeur the opening of [Hyperion]' . 'We now take leave of Mr Keats with wonder at the gigantic stride he has taken, and with the good hope that, if he proceeds in the high and pure style he has now chosen, he will attain an exalted and a lasting station among English poets'.

Meanwhile, Shelley, who had received news from the Gisbornes about Keats's illness, wrote to him from Pisa in July. The letter demonstrated Shelley's good-heartedness in his offer to care for Keats in Pisa, but other aspects of the letter including a reference to the poor sales of 'Endymion', and his advice to Keats to 'avoid system and mannerism' seem spectacularly ill-judged.

As Shelley's letter was making its way from Italy to London an unfortunate incident had led Keats to leave Hunt's house. A letter to him from Fanny Brawne had been handed to a maid who had just given her notice. However, she failed to pass it on and when it was later given to Keats its seal had been broken. He took it badly, decided he was no longer welcome at Hunt's, packed up his few books and belongings, and set off to friends nearby. He ended up however at the Brawnes' apartments, and Mrs Brawne, seeing his condition, took him in. At last he was with his girl.

But not for long. Plans were now being made for Keats to travel to Rome, to be in a warmer climate and be under the care of the respected doctor James Clark. As Keats was apologising to Hunt for his abrupt departure over the letter – Hunt replied assuring him that 'you must have seen by this time how much I am attached to yourself' – he was also responding to Shelley's letter. Described by Andrew Motion as 'vulnerable but determined', he replied on the 16th August.

If Shelley's letter to Keats was marred by condescension and misunderstanding, Keats's reply also jars. Without having read 'Prometheus Unbound', and by his own admission returning Shelley's (ill-conceived) advice from years before to him, he maintains Shelley should still be working on it, and 'loading every rift with ore'.

Despite the fact that the letters seem like ships passing in the night, and Keats was again declining Shelley's offer of hospitality, he was still holding out the possibility of meeting up again, unless 'prevented by a circumstance I have very much at heart to prophesy'. And he seems to have appreciated the consideration shown by Shelley, writing around the 20th August: 'Last week I received a letter from Shelley, of a very kind nature, asking him to spend the winter with him'. He also mentioned Leigh Hunt, noting that 'Hunt has behaved very kindly to me'.

In Ravenna Keats was also on Byron's mind. Murray had sent him a copy of his new book, and his reaction was harsh in the extreme:

'Here are Johnny Keats's piss a-bed poetry [...] There is such trash of Keats and the like upon my tables, that I am ashamed to look at them [...] No more Keats, I entreat: flay him alive; if some of you don't I must skin him myself: there is no bearing the driveling idiotism of the Mankin'.

Later, when he saw the Edinburgh Review's favourable treatment of the 1820 poems, he wrote:

'The *Edinburgh* praises Jack Keats or Ketch, or whatever his names are [...] why, his is the Onanism of Poetry…the outstretched poesy of this miserable Self-polluter of the human mind'.

And later he explained:

'Mr Keats, whose poetry you enquire after, appears to me what I have already said: such writing is a sort of mental masturbation – he is always frigging his Imagination. I don't mean he is indecent, but viciously soliciting his ideas into a state, which is neither poetry nor anything else but a Bedlam vision produced by raw pork and opium'.

But these would not be his last words on Keats.

At the beginning of the year Keats's brother George had returned from America in some financial distress, and drained the available family funds in a confused transaction; Keats's friends reacted indignantly but George was clear in his own mind that he had acted correctly. The end result though, was that Keats was left with virtually no resources. As he would write in a simple will: 'My chest of books divide among my friends. … All my estate real and personal consists in the sale of books publish'd or unpublished'.

George had said as he left: 'You, John, have so many friends, they will be sure to take care of you!', and in the first weeks of September they were indeed busying themselves preparing his journey to Italy. The painter Joseph Severn had agreed to be his travelling companion and carer, John Taylor deposited £150 in a bank in Rome, and his devoted friend William Haslam organised berths on a Naples-bound ship, the Maria Crowther. And so it came to pass that on the 13th September Fanny Brawne wrote in a copy of Hunt's Literary Pocket Book that Keats had given her: 'Mr Keats left Hampstead'.

The journey to Naples would be Keats's last encounter with Byron, in the shape of the first two cantos of

'Don Juan' which he had packed with his few belongings. Severn did not record any adverse response to Byron's caricature of the archetypal Romantic poet:

> He pored upon the leaves, and on the flowers,
> And heard a voice in all the winds; and then
> He thought of wood-nymphs and immortal bowers,
> And how the goddesses came down to men:
> He missed the pathway, he forgot the hours,
> And when he looked upon his watch again,
> He found how much old Time had been a winner—
> He also found that he had lost his dinner.

But he did, according to Severn, object strongly to Byron's description of Juan's shipwreck, which included an incident of cannibalism. It's tempting to think that the exact point at which Keats finally lost patience was when the crew was contemplating one of their number as a potential meal, but changed their minds when they discovered that he had contracted a sexually transmitted disease.

> And next they thought upon the master's mate,
> As fattest; but he saved himself, because,
> Besides being much averse from such a fate,
> There were some other reasons: the first was,
> He had been rather indisposed of late;
> And that which chiefly proved his saving clause
> Was a small present made to him at Cadiz,
> By general subscription of the ladies.

'Keats threw down the book and exclaimed: 'This gives me the most horrid view of human nature, that a man like Byron should have exhausted all the pleasures of the world so completely that there was nothing left for him but to laugh and gloat over the most solemn and heart-rending scenes of human misery; this storm of his is one of the most diabolical attempts ever made on our sympathies, and I have no doubt that it will fascinate thousands into extreme obduracy of heart – the tendency of Byron's poetry is based on a paltry originality, that of making solemn things gay and gay things solemn'.

And that (if Severn's account is accurate) was his last word on Byron.

On 29th October, a week after the Maria Crowther had arrived in Naples, and as Keats was miserably enduring a period of quarantine on board, Shelley wrote to Leigh Hunt's wife Marianne, informing her that 'Keats's new volume is arrived, & the fragment called Hyperion promises for him that he is destined to become one of the first writers of the age'.

For the rest of his days Shelley would champion Keats wherever he could. Mary Shelley's journal records that him reading 'Hyperion' aloud one evening, and in November he wrote to Peacock, alerting him to its merits: 'I dare say you have not time to read it; but it is certainly an astonishing piece of writing, and gives me a conception of Keats which I confess I had not before'. Peacock, though, would respond dismissively: 'If I should live to the age of Methusalem, and have uninterrupted leisure, I should not find time to read Keats's 'Hyperion'. Shelley though, was determined to broaden his mind, responding: 'if the

Hyperion be not grand poetry, none has been produced by our contemporaries'.

He also drafted but never sent a letter to William Gifford, the editor of the *Quarterly Review*, again championing 'Hyperion' and rebuking him for that magazine's review of 'Endymion'. This he said, 'at least greatly contributed' to the 'embittering of his existence & inducing a disease from which there are now but faint hopes of his recovery'.

In November, on the 11th, he was writing to Leigh Hunt: 'Where is Keats now? I am anxiously expecting him in Italy, when I shall take care to bestow every possible attention on him. I consider his a most valuable life, and I am deeply interested in his safety. I intend to be a physician both of his body and his soul, to keep the one warm, and to teach the other Greek and Spanish. I am aware, indeed, in part, that I am nourishing a rival who will far surpass me; and this is an additional motive, and will be an added pleasure'.

But he had still to find a way into Keats's other works, including his great odes. He had told Marianne Hunt 'His other things are imperfect enough, & what is worse written in the bad sort of style which is becoming fashionable naming those who fancy they are imitating Hunt and Wordsworth'. His unsent letter to Gifford noted that 'the canons of taste to which Keats has conformed in his other compositions are the very reverse of my own'.

Like Keats, Shelley had also taken notice of the storm scene in 'Don Juan'. Writing to Byron earlier in the year, he had commented: 'What a strange and terrible storm is that at sea, and the two fathers, how true, yet how strong a contrast! ... Dante hardly exceeds it'. 'The love letter, and the account of its being written, is altogether a masterpiece of portraiture … Where did you learn all these secrets? I should like to go to school there'.

However, though he did not react prudishly to the poem like many of its critics, he also had reservations about the mordant aspect of the poem – Byron's tactic of eliciting the reader's sympathy, and then undercutting it with a cynical thought. Writing of the use of Donna Julia's farewell letter to Juan by the starving crew, as a means of drawing lots to choose a first victim to be eaten, he said 'I cannot say I equally approve of the service to which this letter was appropriated; or that I think the bitter mockery of our common nature, of which this is one of the expressions, quite worthy of your genius'. In the end he saw the 'power and beauty and wit' of the poem as redeeming 'all this – chiefly because they belie and refute it. Perhaps it is foolish to wish there had been nothing to redeem'.

It would be 'the bitter mockery of our common nature' that would come to strain Byron and Shelley's friendship over the next year and a half. In addition, the hardening of Byron's attitude to Claire, and his apparent violation of the arrangement by which Claire was allowed to see her, called for all Shelley's diplomatic skills as he fought Claire's corner. His two letters to Byron in 1820 had both been about Allegra, sparked by Byron's annoyance at Claire's letters. In the second one, written from Pisa in September, he had tried to take the heat out of the disagreement: 'You are conscious of performing your duty to Allegra, & your refusal to allow her to visit Claire at this distance you conceive to be part of your duty. That Claire should wish to see her is natural. That her disappointment should vex her, & her vexation make her write absurdly is all in the usual order of things'.

Shelley's relationship with Byron was already complicated enough, with personal and intellectual differences that would lead the Byron scholar Peter Cochran to describe them as 'radical incompatibles'. The delicate game he was forced to play with Byron over Allegra was about to acquire another dimension, with his great friend Leigh Hunt, now the only member of the group left in England, 'pensioned and drawn' (as a journalist would put it) to Italy. Shelley would soon be mediating on behalf of Hunt as well as Claire – a game of three-dimensional chess.

By the end of the year Keats was in Rome, staying in an apartment off the Spanish Steps, cared for by Severn and Dr James Clark, who, Keats wrote at the end of November, 'is very attentive to me'. He thought 'there is very little the matter with my lungs, but my stomach, he says, is very bad'. That was the exact reverse of the truth, but as there were no antibiotics to treat tuberculosis at the time, even an accurate diagnosis would have made little difference.

In this last known letter, to Charles Brown, he wrote of his love for Fanny Brawne; 'There is one thought enough to kill me; I could have been well, healthy, alert, &c, walking with her....'; of poetry –'the knowledge of contrast, of light and shade, all that information (primitive sense) necessary for a poem...'; of his sister – 'she walks about my imagination like a ghost', and of his regrets – 'If I recover, I will do all in my power to correct the mistakes made during sickness; and if not, all my faults will be forgiven'. The letter ended 'I can scarcely bid you goodbye, even in a letter. I always made an awkward bow. God bless you! John Keats'.

11

'Now in the realm of light'

At the beginning of 1821 Keats was enduring his last days in the apartment off the Spanish Steps in Rome, asking when his 'posthumous existence' would end, and leaving any letters that came unopened, not bearing to look at them.

Shelley's concern for Keats was seen through his correspondence of the time. In February he wrote to Claire Clairemont, noting that 'Keats is very ill at Naples', but he rowed back on his previous offer to accommodate him. 'I have written to him to ask him to come to Pisa, without however inviting him into our own house. We are not rich enough for that sort of thing…'

Leigh Hunt was also expressing his worries, writing to Shelley 'Poor Keats! They sent word from Rome that he is dying; and he is so fearfully sensitive he cannot even bear to receive news from England, but I hope to the last'. With this understanding of Keats's state of mind Hunt wrote to Severn, asking him to convey his best thoughts:

'Tell that poet and noble-hearted man – that we shall all bear his memory in the most precious part of our hearts, and that the world shall bow their heads to it, as our loves do. Or if this, again, will trouble his spirit, tell him that we shall never cease to remember and love him; and that the most sceptical of us has faith enough in the high things that nature puts into our heads to think all who are of one accord in mind and heart are journeying into one and the same place, and shall unite somewhere or other again, face to face, mutually conscious, mutually delighted. Tell him he is only before us on the road…'

A few weeks later Shelley wrote to Tom Medwin: 'I hear Keats is in Rome, and dangerously ill. Should you happen to see him, or if you could take the trouble to call on him, I should be very glad to know how he is, & where he directs his motions. - & that you say everything that is kind from me to him, & entreat to know if I can be in any manner be of service to him. I am afraid poor fellow that it is too late'.

Indeed it was. Both Hunt and Shelley had been writing weeks after Keats's death on February 23rd. He was already buried in the Protestant (or strictly speaking the non-Catholic cemetery) by the city walls, having asked that the inscription on his tombstone should simply read 'Here lies one whose name was writ in water'.

News of Keats's death arrived in Pisa, in mid-April, through a letter from Hunt. Shelley had been on a visit to Livorno when it arrived, along with one from Byron responding angrily to a recent protest from Claire regarding his decision to place Allegra in a convent north of Ravenna. This had infuriated Claire, who had told Byron he was violating the verbal agreement between them that Allegra would never be separated from one of her parents; 'I therefore represent to you that the putting of Allegra, at her years, in a convent is to me a serious and deep affliction'. She continued by arguing forcefully that education in Italian convents produced women characterised by 'ignorance and profligacy', and that Byron was not only depriving their daughter of 'the protection and friendship of her parents' friends' but forcing 'the adoption of a different religion' on her, as well as 'an education known to be contemptible'.

Shelley sat down straight away to reply to Byron's angry response, exercising the type of diplomacy that frequently leads diplomats to be accused of double dealing. Firstly he took Byron's side against Claire, saying that her letters (which he did not seen) were likely to be provoking and unreasonable, and went on to say that he and Mary thought 'your conduct towards Allegra' had been 'most irreproachable'. But he also tried to soften Byron's antagonism towards Claire, arguing that her anger was, after all, a result of maternal affection, even if 'misguided'. He concluded by planting the thought that perhaps a different solution might be found for Allegra: 'Mary unites with me also in expression of the greatest interest for Allegra; and if circumstances should ever occur, to induce you to change your present plans respecting her, she intreats you to believe that she is most anxious to show it'.

With the letter from Hunt before him he finished by giving the news of Keats's death: 'Young Keats, whose *Hyperion* showed so great a promise, died lately at Rome from the consequences of breaking a blood-vessel, in paroxysms of despair at the contemptuous attack on his book, in the *Quarterly Review*'.

Byron's replied about ten days later, firstly referring to Allegra: 'The child continues doing well, and the accounts are regular and favorable. It is gratifying to me that you and Mrs Shelley do not disapprove of the step which I have taken, which is merely temporary'.

Then, on Keats, he wrote: 'I am very sorry to hear what you say of Keats – is it actually true? I did not think criticism had been so killing … I read the review of "Endymion" in the Quarterly. It was severe, – but surely not so severe as many reviews in that and other journals upon others. I recollect the effect on me of the Edinburgh on my first poem; it was rage, and resistance, and redress – but not despondency nor despair. I grant that those are not amiable feelings; but, in this world of bustle and broil, and especially in the career of writing, a man should calculate upon his powers of resistance before he goes into the arena'.

Byron's scepticism about Shelley's account of Keats's death was entirely justified. As Richard Holmes put it: 'It is transparent … that Shelley was not thinking in any realistic way about Keats's reaction to a review of 1818, but rather of his own reaction to the *Quarterly Review*'s attack on himself in 1819'. This misunderstanding would lead to the flawed but powerful poem Shelley would write in memory of Keats at the beginning of June.

Just as John Lennon was the first of the four Beatles to die, and so break the charmed circle of four, so Keats was the first of the 19th century group to pass on and similarly fracture what can be seen in retrospect as their collective creative endeavour. And just as Paul McCartney and George Harrison wrote elegiac songs for their fallen friend – 'Here Today' and 'All Those Years Ago' – so Shelley would sit down to write his elegy, 'Adonais', which took its cue from Keats's advice – 'be more of an artist and load every rift of your subject with ore'. 'It is a highly wrought piece of art' he would write to the Gisbornes later, 'perhaps better in point of composition than any thing I have written'. He would tell other correspondents that 'Adonais' was 'the least imperfect of my compositions', and 'I confess I would be surprised if that poem were born to an immortality of oblivion'.

His confidence about 'Adonais' was perhaps due to the advice that Keats had given him. 'I know what to think of Adonais' he wrote, 'but what to think of those who confound it with them many bad poems of the day, I know not'.

'Adonais' has more similarities with George's song in memory of John rather than Paul's – it begins with a similar sense of anger at how their friends had been treated by the world, the same anger at their murderers, actual or presumed. George described his killer as in league with the devil, whose offence had caused immeasurable grief. Shelley prefaces 'Adonais' with a verse he took from the 'Lament for Bion' by the Sicilian poet Moschus, which had accused the murderer of the poet Bion of having 'no music in his soul'.

> Poison came, you did know poison,
> Who mixed it for you was so cruel;
> He heard your voice yet gave you venom –
> There was no music in his soul.

'He heard your voice yet gave you venom' – those words, more than two thousand years old, could provide a caption for the photograph of John Lennon, taken five hours before his death, signing his killer's copy of 'Double Fantasy' outside the Dakota building.

Shelley developed the theme of poison and the poisoner in the poem itself:

Our Adonais has drunk poison – oh!
What deaf and viperous murderer could crown
Life's early cup with such a draught of woe?

Just as George pays tribute to Lennon's work, which, he says, had aimed at the truth, and 'imagined it all', Shelley also references Keats's work: the morning, the thunder, the 'pale ocean' and the wild winds:

All he had loved, and moulded into thought,
From shape, and hue, and odour, and sweet sound,
Lamented Adonais. Morning sought
Her eastern watch-tower, and her hair unbound,
Wet with the tears which should adorn the ground,
Dimmed the aereal eyes that kindle day;
Afar the melancholy thunder moaned,
Pale Ocean in unquiet slumber lay,
And the wild Winds flew round, sobbing in their dismay.

And like George who sees Lennon as being in a purer, even enviable state, Shelley also argues for that consoling thought:

He has outsoared the shadow of our night;
Envy and calumny and hate and pain,
And that unrest which men miscall delight,
Can touch him not and torture not again;
From the contagion of the world's slow stain
He is secure....

Paul's song for John, 'Here Today', concentrates on their shared humanity, rivalry, closeness and distance, a relationship undoubtedly as deeply freighted as that between Keats and Shelley. He described it later as a 'memories song', referring to the close pre-Beatles experience of hitch-hiking with John to the Isle of Wight, a storm-enforced break in Key West which turned into 'the night we cried', and finally a deliberate break with the taboo on men declaring love for each other. It raises the possibility that Shelley, if he had lived, might have added something more personal to his writings on Keats, something like the reflective 'On Fanny Godwin', drawing on a memory for inspiration.

In the end 'Here Today' and 'All Those Years Ago' are in the tradition of the memorial poem or song for a beloved and significant poet/musician. The 2nd century 'Lament for Bion', reveals its ancestry:

Dolefully sound, ye groves and Dorian waters,
Lament, ye rivers, our beloved Bion;
Mourn, all ye plants, and whisper low, ye forests;
Ye flowers, breathe sadly from your drooping petals;
Put on deep red, anemones and roses;
Wail thine own letters, hyacinth, and ai ai
Write double on thy leaves for our sweet poet.

Begin the grief, begin, Sicilian Muses.
Ye nightingales, in the thick leafage sobbing,
Tell the Sicilian streams of Arethusa

Bion is dead, the shepherd–boy, and with him
Song too is dead, and all the Dorian music.

There is also Milton, writing in the mid-17th century,
grieving over a lost friend:

For Lycidas is dead, dead ere his prime,
Young Lycidas, and hath not left his peer.
Who would not sing for Lycidas? He knew
Himself to sing, and build the lofty rhyme.
He must not float upon his watery bier
Unwept, and welter to the parching wind,
Without the meed of some melodious tear.

In the end, were not George Harrison's and Paul
McCartney's songs unconscious echoes of this poetic
tradition, moving it into the format of popular song?

By the middle of June Shelley was writing to Claire
(who had met Keats years before at Hunt's house) with news
of his poem: 'My elegy on him is finished: I have dipped my
pen in consuming fire to chastise his destroyers; otherwise
the tone of the poem is solemn and exalted'. He told her that
he was having copies privately printed in Pisa, and added 'I
have received a most melancholy account of the illness of
poor Keats, which I shall neither tell you nor send you; for
it would make you too low-spirited'.

Perhaps this account also contained details of
Keats's request that the inscription on his tomb should
simply read: 'Here lies one whose name was writ in water'
– an inscription which led to one of the only joint

compositions in the Younger Romantics' story. Wanting to give Keats's phrase a positive spin he wrote a supplementary verse, adding to and completing the line as the surviving Beatles would add to and complete Lennon's demos 'Free as a bird', 'Real Love' and 'Now And Then' after his death:

FRAGMENT ON KEATS
WHO DESIRED THAT ON HIS TOMB BE INSCRIBED

'Here lieth One whose name was writ in water'
But, ere the breath that could erase it blew,
Death, in remorse for that fell slaughter,
Death, the immortalising winter, flew
Athwart the stream, - and time's printless torrent grew
A scroll of crystal, blazoning the name
Of Adonais!

'Adonais' was printed by mid-July, with a local friend John Taaffe saving Shelley some embarrassment by persuading him to edit out some overly-personal passages in the preface. 'You were right' Shelley wrote to him: 'I have cancelled in the preface the whole passage relating to my private wrongs'.

While most of the print run remained in sheets to be sent to Ollier in London to be bound in book form, Shelley had some copies made for distribution to friends. Soon a copy of 'Adonais', elegantly printed with 'the types of Didot', was on its way to Byron in Ravenna, with a letter almost apologising for its ardent tone. 'I need not be told that I have been carried too far by the enthusiasm of the moment; by my pity, and my indignation, in panegyric. But if I have erred, I console myself by reflecting that it is in defence of the weak – not in conjunction with the powerful'.

Later he would tell Leigh Hunt in Pisa 'that he had written the Elegy in too melancholy a spirit, but that he was too strongly affected during the composition with a sense of what he himself had endured, & that it was more an elegy on himself than the subject of it'.

After 'Adonais' had arrived in Ravenna Byron asked John Murray 'are you aware that Shelley has written an elegy on Keats – and accuses the Quarterly of killing him?' It was all grist to his mill, and he included two verses in his letter:

Who killed John Keats?
I, says the Quarterly
So savage & Tartarly
'Twas one of my feats –

Who shot the arrow?
The poet-priest Milman
(So ready to kill man)
Or Southey or Barrow. –

'You know very well that I did not approve of Keats's poetry or principles of poetry – or of his abuse of Pope – but as he is dead – omit all that is said about him in any M.S.S. of mine – or publication. – His Hyperion is a fine monument & will keep his name – I do not envy the man – who wrote the article – your review people have no more right to kill than any other foot pads. – However – he who

141

would die of an article in a review – would probably have died of something else equally trivial…'

So Byron had moved from his outright condemnation of Keats and all his works to an acceptance that 'Hyperion' did indeed have merit. He confirmed this to Shelley that summer: 'the impression of 'Hyperion' on my mind – is – that it was the best of his works'.

Later he would include in 'Don Juan' some more reflections on Keats:

> John Keats, who was killed off by one critique,
>   Just as he really promised something great,
>   If not intelligible, -- without Greek
>   Contrived to talk about the Gods of late,
>   Much as they might have been supposed to speak.
>   Poor fellow! His was an untoward fate:--
> 'Tis strange the mind, that very fiery particle,
> Should let itself be snuffed out by an Article.

Most of his letter to Shelley is now lost, but it contained an urgently worded invitation to Ravenna, for his residence there was drawing to a close.

At the end of July Teresa's father and brother, both members of the Carbonari, had been exiled from Ravenna due to their political activities, and Teresa had left with them. As they waited in Florence Byron wanted Shelley's advice as to where he, and they, could relocate. It was an invitation that would bring the two poets into closer contact than ever before, with Hunt drawn into a plan that Byron proposed, and Shelley – wanting to see his friend on Italian soil and hopefully rescue his finances – making every effort to bring to fruition. A new adventure was beginning.

Shelley's first impressions of Ravenna were relayed to Mary the morning after he had arrived, on August 7th. 'I arrived last night at 10 o clock and sate up …talking with Lord Byron till 5 this morning…' He was, said Shelley, 'very well, & was delighted to see me' as well as living 'a life totally the reverse of that which he led at Venice … he is now quite well and immersed in politics and literature'. All this was due to his new liaison with Teresa, who had unequivocally rescued him from his Venetian excesses. 'The connexion with la Guiccioli has been an inestimable benefit to him'.

They had not seen each other for nearly two years – now the two poets' friendship renewed. 'Our manner of life is this' Shelley wrote to Mary. 'LB gets up at two – breakfasts – we read talk &c. until six then we ride & dine at eight, and after dinner sit talking till four or five in the morning'.

They discussed Allegra, who 'he says, is grown very beautiful: but he complains that her temper is violent and imperious. I have not yet seen her, but shall tomorrow or next day, as I shall ride over to Bagnacavallo for that purpose'.

Of course they discussed their work as well: 'He has read to me one of the unpublished cantos of Don Juan (Canto V) which is astonishingly fine. It sets him not above but far above all the poets of the day: every word has the stamp of immortality. – I despair of rivalling Lord Byron…'

Part of their discussions must have revolved around the extraordinary attack on Shelley and Byron by the poet laureate Robert Southey. Byron already suspected Southey of spreading those 'league of incest' rumours after their summer on Lake Geneva. Though Southey always denied involvement his animosity to the younger poets had spilled out earlier in the year. In February, he had made his feelings about Byron and 'Don Juan' all too clear in a letter to Walter Savage Landor:

'A fashion of poetry has been imported, which has had a great run, and is in a fair way of being worn out. In his sportive way, Frere began it … Lord Byron followed; first with his Beppo, which implied the profligacy of the writer, and, lastly, with his Don Juan, which is a foul blot on the literature of the country, an act of high treason on English poetry'.

He then went public with his polemic when he had published 'A Vision of Judgement', an account, in hexameters, of the reception of the recently deceased George III into heaven. In its preface he suddenly broke off an arcane discussion on hexameters, 'Latin versification' and 'the native spondee' to launch a wild assault on the 'lewdness and impiety' of recent English poetry.

It was an obvious attack on Byron and Shelley in particular: 'The publication of a lascivious book is … a sin … no after repentance in the writer can counteract. Whatever remorse of conscience he may feel when his hour comes (and come it must!) will be of no avail. The poignancy of a death-bed repentance cannot cancel one copy of the thousands which are sent abroad ….' They were 'men of diseased hearts and depraved imaginations ... The school which they have set up may properly be called the Satanic school ... Let the rulers of the state look to this, in time!

So Southey characterised them as 'the Satanic School' and called for the British state to monitor and indict them, presumably under the charge of blasphemous libel that was in frequent use at the time.

'These calumnies' Shelley would write to Mary shortly before leaving Ravenna, 'have ultimately for object the depriving us of the means of security & subsistence. You will easily perceive the gradations by which calumny proceeds to pretext, pretext to persecution, and persecution to the ban of fire & water'. Faced with this, Shelley told Mary that 'my greatest content would be utterly to desert all human society. I would retire with you & our child to a solitary island in the sea, would build a boat, and shut upon my retreat the floodgates of the world. I would read no reviews and talk with no authors'. Given that this was not a particularly realistic prospect 'The other side of the alternative ... is to form for ourselves a society of our own class, as much as possible, in intellect or in feelings ... Our roots were never struck as deeply as at Pisa...'

So in Ravenna the two poets were planning their response, with Byron's long-imagined plan for a journal now acquiring new impetus. Byron's difficulties could be solved by moving to the more liberal Pisa; Teresa and her family could all find sanctuary there; Hunt's fortunes would benefit from being its editor; Byron would have an outlet for his response to Southey, and Shelley would be, at long last, be reunited with his friend.

So soon Shelley was writing to Mary: 'Lord Byron is immediately coming to Pisa – he will set off immediately I can get him a house. Who would have imagined it! ... One thing' he continued, 'with Lord Byron & the people we know at Pisa we should have a security & protection ....'

Shelley was still rooting for Allegra – 'One thing of great consequence however; & which cannot be thought of too soon is Allegra - & what is to be done with her'. Could Mary think of anyone in Pisa who would look after her, could she think of a maid to accompany her from the convent to Pisa?

On his return to Pisa he took a lease on a palazzo on the Arno, the Palazzo Lanfranchi, and wrote to Byron about the logistics of the move, the possibility that Allegra could find a new home in Pisa, and also on 'The Prophecy of Dante'. A 'professed critic' in Pisa he said, was 'in raptures' with it, and added that 'the poetry of this piece is indeed sublime'. He thought, though, that 'it will only be fully appreciated by the select readers of many generations'; as he was being forced to the conclusion that his own work faced a similar fate, it was another example of his kinship with Byron.

He also wrote to Hunt, informing him of the planned journal, and inviting him to Italy. After Hunt had agreed to make the move he confirmed to him that 'Lord Byron is expected very day & I know will be delighted to hear of your coming'. In the same letter he gave some travel advice that would have fateful consequences: 'You would do well to come by sea instead of crossing France at this season of the year'.

But Byron was dawdling in Ravenna, writing his 'Detached Thoughts' in his emptying rooms as Teresa waited anxiously for him in Pisa. 'When may we expect you?' Shelley wrote in late October. He was still hoping that Allegra could be brought to Pisa, despite the fact that 'the Countess tells me you think of leaving (her) for the present in the convent. Do as you think best, - but I can pledge myself to find a situation for her here such as you would approve....'

Keats was still on Shelley's mind. 'I should very much like to hear what is said of my Adonais' he wrote to John Gisborne in October, also telling him that he was 'just finishing a dramatic poem called Hellas upon the contest now waging in Greece'.

At last Byron arrived, in early November. 'Lord Byron is established here, and we are constant companions. No small relief this, after the dreary solitude of the understanding and the imagination in which we passed the first years of our expatriation, yoked to all sorts of miseries and discomforts'.

Later that month Shelley wrote to Joseph Severn, enclosing a copy of 'Adonais', referring to Keats's 'transcendent genius' and adding that he hardly thought 'when I last saw Keats at my friend Leigh Hunt's, that I should survive him'.

12
An Italian Apple

'Apple was a noble experiment that failed', wrote Richard DiLello in his account of the Apple years. You could say the same thing about the journal that Byron, Shelley and Hunt set up in Pisa in 1822. Eventually named *The Liberal*, it would fail to get established, and for years was regarded as a critical and financial failure.

However, in the longer term both Apple and the Romantics have made their mark, both critically and financially. Yoko Ono, once asked about the 'failure' of Apple Corps, was having none of it. She reminded the interviewer that Apple had turned out to be the vehicle for supporting each Beatle and maintaining the group's legacy. 'I don't call that a failure' she said. With reported earnings of £50m in 2018 it was clearly a going concern, and Apple still produces significant, critically-acclaimed and popular Beatles projects. Back in the 19th century *The Liberal* may have ceased publication after four issues but the Romantics' larger project still continues. The economic legacy of the Romantics may not be so readily audited, but it still must be considerable, when global scholarship, education, publishing, conferences, tourism and other factors are taken into account. So though the initial high hopes for each project may not have succeeded, each have, in their way, found a place in the 'dull dense world', with *The Liberal*, as will be seen, being rehabilitated over time.

A comparison between the two projects gives a sense of how 'the creative industries' have developed over the 150 years that separate them. The Beatles had a management team and support in the areas of finance, graphics, publicity – all capitalizing on their global recognition, enabled by the new mass media technology.

Though Brian Epstein could make mistakes on the business side of things, his achievement had been to package and present them, but also to give them a trusted and principled environment in which they could flourish. According to Cynthia Lennon, when The Beatles stopped touring and Brian Epstein's role as manager and promoter came to a shuddering halt, he had dreamed up the idea of a new creative and merchandising entity that would involve him and the boys in a new venture. After his death it was financial momentum that kept his idea alive – their accountant told them the pot of money they had could go in tax or they could do something with it. They chose the latter option: Apple was to be an umbrella organisation with each Beatle having would have their own creative outlet within it. Apple would produce films, records, books, electronics, and give opportunities to creative souls stifled by 'the system'. There would also be an Apple shop on Baker St.

Though the Romantics' project did not have the resources enjoyed by The Beatles such resources they did have levers to pull – Leigh Hunt would supply editorial expertise and publishing facilities through his brother John, Byron's celebrity was always a giant plus, and Shelley would be able to contribute through diplomacy and with contributions to its pages. However, the financing was uncertain, being largely dependent on Byron. They had no back up team of managers, publicists, accountants. Yet the impulse was much the same: with *The Liberal*, there would be an attempt to create a progressive community in Pisa, to establish an outlet that would give them and other liberal writers a mouthpiece (Hunt was extremely well connected in this regard), enable Byron to reply to his numerous critics – he was still infuriated by Southey's 'Satanic School' attack – and doubtless to provide a platform for political comment.

'Byron-mania' was still a force; on the way to Pisa from Ravenna, when he had passed through a Florence full of English visitors, heads turned. It was nearly a decade after 'Childe Harold', but he still had a Beatles-like pulling power. 'I wish you had seen him set off' wrote his friend Samuel Rogers to his sister, 'every window of the inn was open to see him'. So in Pisa, after he had refused an invitation to visit the Grand Duke of Tuscany, the Grand Duke actually rode to Byron's palace to try to get a glimpse of Pisa's famous resident.

If Shelley's letter inviting Keats to Pisa had borne fruit, and if he had indeed recovered (perhaps due to local doctor Andrea Vacca's expertise) one can, perhaps, speculate about his possible involvement in the project. With Byron's new-found respect for his 'Hyperion' he and Byron might have been able to arrive at some kind of rapprochement. Shelley might have persuaded Keats that Byron poems like 'Manfred' and 'The Prophecy of Dante' were in a different league to the scorned Augustan poetic style he so disliked, and so all four would have been present in Pisa, no doubt all contributing to *The Liberal*, and forming a proto-Beatles in the early 19th century! All gathering at the Palazzo Lanfranchi on the Lung' Arno in Pisa, a building not unlike the Apple HQ at 3 Savile Row in London.

Even before *The Liberal* had begun to publish it was making news. Wordworth's horror at the plan has already been noted, Byron's friends in London worried that Byron's reputation would be dragged down by his association with 'this vicious set in Pisa', and the journalist John Watkins was able to add a new section to his new book on Byron. According to him 'his Lordship's [establishment of] a literary circle at Pisa ... has a most portentous aspect. Thus the charge of his having formed a poetical school of immorality and profaneness, will, there is reason to fear, be realized in the literal sense, and to the fullest extent. This college of infidelity, founded, supported and directed by the noble Lord, under his own roof, will no doubt make a considerable noise in the world'.

Apple Records had started off with two hits – 'Hey Jude' by The Beatles themselves and 'Those were the Days' by Mary Hopkin. For their part the Romantics planned to lead off with Byron's satire 'The Vision of Judgement', the riposte to Southey, which was bound to be a veritable *succès de scandale.*

The expectation was that the first edition of the journal could be produced in the New Year and that the 'little nest of singing birds' in Pisa would soon be in full voice. 'I expect [Hunt] & his family here every day' Shelley wrote to Joseph Severn at the end of the month. The journal seemed set.

The Shelleys' apartment was five minutes' walk from the Palazzo Lanfranchi, and at first Byron was a welcome relief from the years of isolation in Italy. Byron, with his contacts with the literary world, his stable of horses which enabled rides out to the countryside and pistol practice, his billiard table, his library with the latest journals and magazines from Britain, the weekly dinners which he gave for the menfolk of the 'Pisan Circle' – all these were – at first – welcome diversions for Shelley. He had a regular one hour visit to the Lanfranchi in the afternoons; it was fun, obviously, having Byron around, but his success and celebrity could not help but stir uneasy reactions in Shelley, which only increased as time went by.

Just as Apple Corps proved to be a magnet for sympathetic spirits such as Ken Kesey, assorted Hell's Angels George had encountered in San Francisco, and budding musicians and hangers on, so Byron's presence in Pisa proved an irresistible draw. To the friends of the Shelleys, particularly Ned and Jane Williams who occupied the same apartment block in Pisa, were added Shelley's cousin Thomas Medwin in November, who began taking 'very copious notes' of Byron's conversations and table talk. These included Byron's statement that he was 'forever battling with the Snake [Shelley] about Keats' and another lamentation that 'Shelley can versify better than I'. And the adventurer and writer Edward John Trelawny arrived in mid-January.

One budding inventor, an early version perhaps of Apple's self-styled electronic genius 'Magic Alex', also got in touch. A letter arrived from a mechanic in Bologna, signed 'by a number of professors', asking for Byron to sponsor 'a machine, with which a man, by the aid of wings is to elevate himself to any height – in short to fly. The whole is to be worked by *steam* and … a small body has already been raised by a similar mechanism and made to fly about the room'. Despite the apparent success of this prototype, Byron did not bite; Magic Alex, having become a Lennon confidant, was part of Apple Corps until eventually fired by Allen Klein.

Though a band's songwriters can become much better off than non-songwriting group members, this never seemed to be an issue with The Beatles. In Pisa however, there was a massive financial disparity between Byron and the others. Arriving in Pisa with a staff of eight, a stable of nine horses, a part-time gardener, an accountant who oversaw all outgoings, a penchant for fine linen and a slimmed down menagerie that still included geese, dogs and a monkey, he was the social and financial centre of the Pisan Circle. On him and him alone relied the journal, and around him a social circle developed, with diversions like billiards at the Lanfranchi and expeditions to a nearby farm for pistol practice. Shelley, the son of a baronet and heir to a family estate in East Sussex, had a comfortable income but Byron's was at least five time higher. For the journal to succeed, his involvement was key.

In creative terms though, Shelley and Byron were far more evenly matched. The mighty Byron could find himself humbled by Shelley: 'At this juncture Shelley joined us' wrote Trelawny, telling of an encounter in the Lanfranchi. 'He never laid aside his book and magic mantle; he waved his wand and Byron, after a faint show of defiance, stood mute…. Shelley's earnestness and just criticism held him captive'.

Byron had a defence mechanism though, as Medwin noted: 'Shelley frequently lamented that it was almost impossible to keep him to any one given point. He flew about from subject to subject like a will o' the wisp, touching them with a false fire – with his love of mystification it was impossible to know when he was in earnest. He also dealt, too, in the gross and indelicate of which Shelley had an utter abhorrence…. Byron was so sensible of his inability to cope with [Shelley, in argument] that he always avoided coming to a trial of their strength in controversy, which he generally cut off with a joke or a pun; for Shelley was what Byron could not be, a close, logical, and subtle reasoner'. Leigh Hunt later summed up their differing outlooks: 'Lord Byron thought his philosophy too spiritual and romantic, Mr Shelley thought his Lordship's too material and despairing'.

But if Byron conceded Shelley's poetic excellence – 'he was poetry itself' he said later – his own works certainly held Shelley's attention. Though 'Don Juan' was vastly different from his own work he recognised its merits immediately, calling it 'pregnant with immortality', and in a letter to Byron, written shortly before he arrived in Pisa, he explained exactly why he admired it. Having just received cantos 3 to 5 he told Byron that 'it is totally of its own species', was marked by its 'grace of composition' and 'carries with it at once the stamp of originality and a defiance of imitation'.

He seemed to have changed his mind about what he'd called its 'bitter mockery of our common nature' on the grounds that his depiction of human nature was nothing but the truth: 'You unveil & present in its true deformity what is worst in human nature, and this is what the witlings of the age murmur at'. Contrary to 'the witlings', and going back on his previous reservations about Byron's work, Shelley now saw this as useful and beneficial: 'We are damned to the knowledge of good and evil, and it is well for us to know what we should avoid no less than what we should seek'.

In 1818 Shelley had written some lines to Byron which had attributed to him a Beatles-like influence over the era he lived in:

> O mighty mind, in whose deep stream this age
> Shakes like a reed in the unheeding storm,
> Why dost thou curb not thine own sacred rage?

Now, in January 1822, he wrote his 'Sonnet to Byron', describing his works as 'perfect worlds' and painfully acknowledging his own inferiority.

There was one nagging problem: there was as yet no sign of Leigh Hunt, and violent storms were raging across Europe. In Pisa the worries mounted and finally it was confirmed he had been delayed. As Shelley wrote to his 'Ozymandias' friend Horace Smith: 'Hunt was expected … when we heard that the late violent storms had forced him to put back, & that nothing could persuade Marianne to put to sea again. This for many reasons … has produced a chaos of perplexities'.

The journal, then, had to be put on the back burner, and talk turned to the summer months. The Shelleys usually stayed in the pleasant spa town San Giuliano di Pisa but the idea now was that both Shelley and Byron would decamp for the coast. What was more, Trelawny had a friend in Genoa, Captain Daniel Roberts, who could build them sailing boats in the naval shipyard. Shelley ordered a scaled down version of an American schooner – 'the fastest thing on the water' – and wrote that he 'dreamed of nothing but sailing, and fishing up coral'. Byron trumped him by ordering a grander vessel – 'with no expense to be spared' as Trelawny told Roberts.

'I do not like this idea of a boat' Mary wrote, but the impetus for a summer of sailing was irresistible. Soon Shelley and Williams had located a possible candidate for a summer residence, a large house on the shore in the Gulf of Spezia, opposite the village of Lerici.

At this point the escalating and increasingly bitter warfare between Byron and the poet laureate broke out again. Byron's response to Southey's attempt to brand him the leader of a 'Satanic School' had been published in an appendix to his play 'The Two Foscari' soon after he had arrived in Pisa.

He had scorned Southey's call for 'The Satanic School' to be prosecuted: 'Poor Southey' he wrote, 'has been prattling about "a Satanic School" and recommending it to the "notice of the legislature". Poor fellow! It is sad work to see him reduced to cry upon a Government to help him against a few verses...'

Then Southey's 'death-bed' fantasies came under fire: 'With a cowardly ferocity he exults over the anticipated "death-bed repentance" of the objects of his dislike; and indulges himself In a pleasant "Vision of Judgment", in prose as well as verse, full of impious impudence'.

He concluded by noting how Southey's assaults were hypocritical given the radicalism of his early work: 'There is something at once ludicrous and blasphemous in this arrogant scribbler of all work sitting down to deal damnation and destruction upon his fellow creatures, with Wat Tyler, the Apotheosis of George the Third, and the Elegy on Martin the regicide, all shuffled together in his writing desk'.

In February Southey's response, in the *British Courier* of January 1822, arrived in Pisa.

"Of the work which I have done it becomes me not here to speak, save only as relates to the Satanic School, and its Coryphæus [in Greek drama, the leader of the chorus], the author of Don Juan. I have held up that school to public detestation, as enemies to the religion, the institutions, and the domestic morals of the country. I have given them a designation *to which their founder and leader answers*. I have sent a stone from my sling which has smitten their Goliath in the forehead. I have fastened his name upon the gibbet for reproach and ignominy, as long as it shall endure. Take it down who can!' He finished his diatribe: 'One word of advice to Lord Byron before I conclude. When he attacks me again let it be in rhyme'.

It was Thomas Medwin who showed it to Byron. 'I shall never forget his countenance as he glanced rapidly over the contents. He looked perfectly awful: his colour changed almost prismatically; his lips were pale as death. He said not a word ... He paused a moment, and said: 'You have not seen my Vision of Judgement'.

'The Vision of Judgement' then, was key to Byron's ability to respond to Southey. Murray would not publish it, so if Byron had any reservations about the journal they must have vanished at this point. Indeed, two months later Shelley would write to Hunt: 'He expresses again the greatest eagerness to undertake it and proceed with it, as well as the greatest confidence in you as his associate. He is forever dilating upon his impatience if your delay & his disappointment at your not having already arrived...'

The balance of influence was tipping towards Shelley, with the kind of direction he was encouraging synchronising with the course Byron was now taking. However capricious his Lordship was, however he might gossip to his friends back in London that the journal 'would be an abortion', it was in his interests to go with the flow of events that Shelley was overseeing.

His opponents in Britain sensed the shift in Byron's course: it had been John Murray who had talked of 'the vicious set in Pisa', and Byron's old pal Tom Moore remonstrated with him about linking his fortunes with the seditious Hunt and the atheist Shelley. But Byron was having none of it, replying:

'As to poor Shelley, who is another bugbear to you and the world, he is, to my knowledge, the *least* selfish and the mildest of men—a man who has made more sacrifices of his fortune and feelings for others than any I ever heard of. With his speculative opinions I have nothing in common, nor desire to have. The truth is, my dear Moore, you live near the *stove* of society, where you are unavoidably influenced by its heat and its vapours...'

So Byron was moving from his position as the golden boy of high society publishing to a more marginalised status, and in the process taking a lead from Shelley. This shifting of influence within the group was also a part of The Beatles' career. John Lennon generally dominated the group's early work, but with Sergeant Pepper Paul's influence began to be a powerful counterweight. After Brian Epstein's death it became more pronounced, but George then slipped into a leadership role with the Maharishi and the expedition to Rishikesh. After the critical mauling in the UK of 'The Magical Mystery Tour' Paul's influence waned, but his creativity could not be contained.

A spellbinding aspect of the Peter Jackson 'Get Back' trilogy was to watch Paul coming up with the title song, providing a perfect vehicle for them.

Jackson's film demonstrated the 'perplexities' The Beatles had to negotiate while trying to write an album of songs and make a movie in under a month; the first of the 'perplexities' Shelley was faced with was the need to scrape together £150 to tide Hunt and his family over while he waited in Plymouth for a spring passage. He and Mary had already contributed to the furnishing of his flat at the Lanfranchi, and this was a further drain on their family budget. Later that month he asked Hunt to make sure that he could rely on income from *The Examiner*, as 'many difficulties have presented themselves to the plan imagined by Lord Byron'.

By February Shelley found himself in the awkward position of having to negotiate with Byron for yet more funds for Hunt. He managed to get a loan of £250 from Byron, secured on his inheritance, but it did not help in their already difficult relationship. He told Hunt that 'many circumstances have occurred between myself & Lord B. which make the intercourse painful to me, and this last discussion about money particularly so'.

At this point the immensely problematic issue of Allegra came to the fore. Claire wrote to Byron, Shelley and Mary, and others that she was planning to leave Italy and begged Byron to let her visit her child before her departure.

When she received no satisfactory response she then wrote to Shelley asking him to forge a letter so that she could remove Allegra from the convent. The Shelleys replied that was impossible, and tried to calm Claire's forebodings, without success: she continued writing emotionally charged letters to Byron, leaving Shelley in a supremely difficult position. Though taking Claire's side, he could not afford to alienate Byron completely; that could put the journal – and the reunion with Leigh Hunt – in jeopardy.

Without the uniting factor of the journal there was a sense of being adrift and at the mercy of events. At the end of March Shelley, Byron and their circle of friends were involved in an incident with a dragoon from the local garrison, which ended with the dragoon being stabbed with a pitchfork by one of Byron's servants. He was 'taken to the misericordia, with all bells ringing', and though soon out of danger, a police investigation began into what became known as the 'Masi affair'. Byron's residence in Pisa was at risk.

Then, at the beginning of April, there was a hammer blow: news arrived that Allegra had died of typhus. With Claire due to visit any day Shelley decided to remove her from Byron's proximity and so, after taking 'a tight-lipped leave of Lord Byron who was morosely contemplating his own emigration to Livorno', with Claire, Mary and their young son, and Ned and Jane Williams, they set off for the bay of Lerici. It was there that Claire heard of Allegra's death: 'after the first shock' Shelley wrote to Byron, 'she has sustained her loss with more fortitude than I had dared to hope'. According to Mary, 'Lord Byron felt the loss at first bitterly; he also felt remorse, for he felt that he had acted against everyone's counsels and wishes, and death had stamped with truth the many and often-urged prophecies of Clare…'

A devastating tragedy for Claire, one also has to feel for Mary. Finally, in Pisa, and after years of travelling and upheaval, they had found what looked like a permanent home, a top floor apartment overlooking the Arno. They had furnished it themselves; Shelley had ordered his library of books from England and with Mary pregnant again she could look forward to the birth of another child with all the amenities, creature comforts and medical facilities of the city at hand. Now, after negotiations for a house on the shore, the Casa Magni, were completed, she found herself in a wild and desolate environment, with the family interests being subordinated to the grand project of the journal and Shelley's hopes of benefitting Hunt.

Though Shelley, alert to the dangers of letting things slide, had warned Hunt back in January that his late arrival could jeopardise the project ('the best thing you could do is, without waiting for the spring, to set sail on the very first ship you can') it was not until mid-May that Hunt finally set off. Before he left Plymouth though, there was a reminder that Hunt had his own fan club, and was not to be completely overshadowed by his Lordship the noble poet, the notorious author of 'Queen Mab' or by the deceased author of 'Hyperion'. Local admirers in Plymouth presented him with a fine silver goblet with the inscription 'To Leigh Hunt Esq., in admiration of his long, continued & successful exertions in the cause of FREEDOM, TRUTH AND HUMANITY, his eminent talents and numerous virtues'.

Seven weeks later he arrived in Genoa, seven weeks that for the Shelley household had combined intensity, drama and powerful Shelley poems written in what Mary would call the 'unimaginable beauty' of the bay of Lerici. In addition to his final masterwork 'The Triumph of Life', he wrote haunting shorter poems fused with the beauty of his surroundings and his growing emotional attachment to

Jane Williams. Imbued with, as Nora Crook puts it, a 'desire for an impossible prolongation of fleeting intervals of beauty and joy or regret or their passing', in retrospect they have a sense of impending closure, a poignancy akin to the songs John Lennon was working on in his final days.

Meanwhile the Byron circus had moved to the outskirts of Livorno with the legal proceedings into the Masi imbroglio hanging over him and Teresa's family. Sailing down the coast to Livorno Hunt met up with Trelawny, 'with his knight-errant aspect, dark, handsome and mustachioed', and a day or two later set out for Byron's summer retreat south of Livorno, arriving to find 'the hottest looking house I ever saw'. He walked straight into a domestic crisis. One of Byron's servants had stabbed Teresa's brother Pietro whose arm was in a sling, and the household was in uproar. Teresa, Hunt recalled, was 'flushed and dishevelled, and 'would not hear of the charitable remarks of Lord Byron, who was for making light of the matter'.

'Everything was foreign and vehement' he remembered, with the servant first threatening everyone with his knife but then 'throwing himself on a bench, extending his arms, and bursting into tears'. His final move was to beg Byron to kiss him, but his Lordship 'conceived this excess of charity superfluous… He pardoned him, but said he must not think of remaining in his service'.

Hunt noted how coolly Byron had handled the situation, 'trying to damp all this fire with his cool tones, and an air of voluptuous indolence'. It had been at least eight years since he had seen Byron in London, and he 'scarcely knew [him], as he had grown so fat, and I so thin'. He 'presented a very different aspect from the compact, energetic, and curly haired person I had known in England'.

Shelley's fears that his delayed arrival could imperil their project were being realised – when the local police got wind of the incident it was a further black mark against Byron. Before long news came through that Teresa's family the Gambas had had their residence in Tuscany revoked. Byron would inevitably follow them to be with Teresa; the Pisan 'Apple building' would have to be vacated.

Trelawny wrote that 'Shelley, with his friend Williams, soon came in their boat, scudding into the harbour of Livorno'. For Shelley this was a moment of pure delight, his long-harboured schemes to lure Hunt to Italy had finally come to fruition. He was 'inexpressibly glad' to see him he kept repeating, but he had a major task ahead of him: not only settling Hunt and his family into the Lanfranchi but putting the journal on a sound footing.

The whole project seemed to be in jeopardy. 'Lord Byron is at this moment on the point of leaving Tuscany' he reported back to Mary. 'The Gambas have been exiled and he declares his intention of following their fortunes …every body is in despair and everything in confusion'. 'It is the worst for poor Hunt' he continued, 'as he seems inclined to depart without the necessary explanations and arrangements due to such a situation as Hunt's'. There was the appalling prospect of Hunt and his family being stranded in Italy without financial support.

Hunt's 12-year-old son Thornton later remembered that Shelley 'had grown since he left England. His voice was stronger, his manner more confident and downright….' He spoke out against the angelic image of Shelley that was growing up in Victorian times by noting the atmosphere of 'active movement, vigour and decision that surrounded him' – these qualities would be vital in the days ahead as he tried to establish the literary project.

So Shelley spent a week with Hunt in Pisa, settling him and his family into the ground floor apartment at the Palazzo Lanfranchi, 'assisting us' as his wife Marianne wrote, 'in any and every way'. Negotiations with Byron were difficult though, and dispiriting. Eventually though, there was a settlement: not only would Byron sign over the copyright of 'The Vision of Judgement' for the first issue but would stand as a financial guarantor for Hunt in return for his work on the journal. All was done, they could relax, and after sightseeing in Pisa with Hunt Shelley could return to Lerici with his mission fulfilled. The last day that he was in Pisa Hunt's review of 'Adonais' appeared back home, in *The Examiner*. It contained a fierce attack on Dr Johnson and his professed principles of poetry, as well as on the contemporary critics who had failed to see Keats's promise and were now trying to ignore Shelley's 'Adonais'.

The very last poem Shelley is known to have written, now lost, welcomed Hunt to Italy, beginning, Hunt recalled, with a description of the fireflies that so often enchant Italian evenings. Next day, when Shelley left for Livorno, Hunt lent him his copy of Keats's 1820 volume of poems, a very special copy as Keats himself had presented it to him during his last stay in Kentish Town. Hunt may have been encouraging Shelley to see beyond 'Hyperion' to the other poems: 'His friend had marked, all through the volume, the passages that had pleased him; & he said he would like to read it over again with him…' 'I entreated him, if the weather was violent, not to give way to his daring spirit and venture to sea. He promised me he would not'.

Settling in to his study in the Lanfranchi Hunt set about organizing the journal's first edition. He sent his brother John a contribution to *The Examiner* Byron had given him, wrote to his friend Elizabeth Kent that Byron was enthusiastic about the journal, was giving instructions to Murray to hand the manuscript of his 'Vision' to John for publication, and also that 'Shelley has some excellent MS. ready too'. At long last, the poets' venture was underway.

The next days passed quietly. At Lerici Mary and Jane waited, watching from the balcony of the Casa Magni for the sails of their boat the Don Juan to round the bay. It never came, and 'On the morning of the third day', wrote Trelawny, 'I rode to Pisa, told my fears to Hunt'. 'I experienced one of the sensations we read of in books' Hunt recalled, 'I was tongue-tied with horror'. Trelawny then 'went upstairs to Byron. When I told him his lip quivered, and his voice faltered as he questioned me'.

They could not have set out, could they, on the day of that terrible summer storm? There was no news. Byron funded a search along the coast, and eventually, after hearing that three bodies had been brought to shore and buried in the dunes by fishermen, Trelawny identified one, near Viareggio, as that of Shelley. In his jacket pocket, 'folded open at 'Lamia', was Hunt's copy of Keats's 1820 poems. 'open, and doubled back, as if it had been thrust in, in the hurry of a surprise'.

Months later, when Shelley's boat the Don Juan was salvaged it was found that its bow was stoved in, a fact that has been seized upon by conspiracy theorists as a sign that his death was far from accidental, but was a deliberate ramming by the Italian authorities who feared the political influence of the group of English expatriates. Or a simple attempt at a sea-going robbery, targeting the money Shelley was bringing back from Livorno.

Such theories are echoed by similar conjectures relating to Lennon's death. Some maintain that the CIA were monitoring John Lennon because of his political activities, trained his killer and supplied him with a bizarre alibi based on J.D. Salinger's novel 'The Catcher in the Rye'. Relaying this theory one blogger declares: 'I firmly believe it was the CIA along with the FBI who murdered John Lennon, because of his distrust of the American government and his hatred for the war'.

In both cases though, the evidence produced for such skullduggery is convoluted and unconvincing. The design of Shelley's boat (open-decked and heavily ballasted) rendered it highly susceptible to sinking if swamped in rough seas. And John Lennon's many fans included some unstable enough to think they could somehow find personal meaning through his murder.

Back on the north-west coast of Italy, as the summer heat built, the scene was set for a performance that would gain, like The Beatles' rooftop concert, an iconic status with the passing of time. The recent release of Peter Jackson's 'Get Back' has been a reminder of how people gathered and were drawn to the Beatles' final concert, hastening towards the sound, looking up from the street, clambering over rooftops to get a glimpse. Trelawny remembered how, as he, Byron and Hunt arrived at the site of Shelley's temporary grave in the sand dunes outside Viareggio, 'there was a considerable   gathering   of   spectators   from   the neighbourhood, and many ladies richly dressed were among them. …The work (of disinterring Shelley's body) went on silently in the deep and unresisting sand, not a word was spoken, for the Italians have a touch of sentiment, and their feelings are easily excited into sympathy'.

And as the cremation on the beach, required by quarantine laws, proceeded, they were all there: the drowned Shelley the centrepiece of the occasion, Leigh Hunt, unable to watch, remaining in the coach, Byron 'silent and thoughtful' according to a Trelawny account (or swimming out to sea according to an earlier version), and John Keats making an appearance when Hunt's copy of his 1820 poems, that Shelley had been reading on his last journey, was thrown into the flames.

It was a partially disembodied gathering perhaps, but in spiritual terms the four poets were as connected as The Beatles had been on the rooftop of 3 Savile Row that cold January day in London. Having first come together over Leigh Hunt's imprisonment ten years earlier, they were now united again on that Italian beach, in spirit if not in body, making a grand performative gesture, as significant in cultural terms as when the opening line of 'I've got a feeling' rang out over the London streets nearly one hundred and fifty years later.

13

'You never give me your money…'

'Mafia here!' the Apple Scruffs would shout as the American businessman Allen Klein's staff pulled up outside the Apple building in Savile Row. Brian Epstein was gone, and Klein's triumphant cry when he heard of his death – 'I've got them' – had been fulfilled. Winning John Lennon over with his intimate knowledge of rock 'n' roll, his apparent insight into Beatle dynamics – 'He knows everything about us' and his proven ability to renegotiate the record deals that had been overwhelmingly favourable to the record companies, he had made his way into The Beatles' organization, securing a three year managerial contract in March 1969. He was now reviewing and calling the shots on Apple Corps and its multifarious activities; only Paul was holding out against him.

A new era had begun, as it had for the remaining Young Romantics in Pisa. A similar bucketful of cold reality had been thrown over the journal and the planned collaboration. 'My heart died within me' Hunt had remembered, thinking back to his reaction to Shelley's death. With Shelley gone there was no one to smooth over the difficulties between Hunt and Byron, no one to think ahead about the journal, no one to raise funds for the project and make it less dependent on Byron (Horace Smith perhaps could have helped), no one to think big about its future. Shelley, though he had said he would not be an active participant in the project, would probably have played a key background role.

However, Byron assured Hunt that 'he would stand in Mr Shelley's place' and Hunt settled into his room on the ground floor of the Lanfranchi and got to work on the first edition of the journal. He left a pleasant account of Byron descending from his rooms upstairs: 'Our manner of life was this. Lord Byron, who used to sit up late at night, writing Don Juan (which he did under the influence of gin and water) rose late in the morning. He breakfasted; read; lounged about, singing an air, and coming down, was heard, still singing in the courtyard, out of which the garden ascended at the back of the house. … I was generally at my writing desk when he came down, and either acknowledged his presence by getting up and saying something from the window, or he called out 'Leontius!' and came halting up to the window with some joke, or other challenge to conversation. We then lounged about, or stayed and talked, Madame Guiccioli with her sleek tresses descending after her toilet to join us'.

All very cordial, and possibly the scene for a recognition by Byron of Keats's poetic genius, as significant perhaps as John Lennon's acknowledgement, in interviews promoting 'Abbey Road', that George Harrison, for so long the junior songwriter in the band, had contributed the best songs to the album. 'It was Lord Byron' wrote Hunt, 'at that time living in Italy, drinking its wine and basking in its sunshine, who asked me what was the meaning of [Keats's] phrase 'a beaker full of the warm south'. Keats's line had showed him something new about poetic possibilities perhaps beyond his own abilities; as Hunt added, 'the sort of poetry in which he excelled, was not used to these poetical concentrations'. The Augustan model had been subverted: John Keats had broken through Lord Byron's guard.

Apple's first, anarchic phase had lasted from John and Paul's New York announcement in January 1968 to Klein's appointment in March 1969. Its second phase, overseen by Klein, would be marked by financial cuts, curbs on expense accounts and extravagant purchases, and brutal sackings of staff. The Apple boutique had been closed long ago, but added to the axed projects were the spoken word label Zapple Records and Apple Electronics. The Magic Alex 'inventions', all of which had failed to get patents, were sold for scrap and Alex was locked out of his workshop. The roster of artists was pruned, and according to Apple executive Peter Brown 'the feeling of joy that had once pervaded the building descended into gloom. ... Three Savile Row had turned into a mausoleum just waiting for a death'.

There was a similar feeling about the final phase of the collaboration, in Genoa, between Byron and Hunt. They were in two separate houses, with Mary and the Hunts a mile away from Byron, who was embarking on a similar regime of financial retrenchment. Leigh Hunt and Mary were disputing the ownership of Shelley's heart, which Trelawny had seized from the funeral pyre and Hunt was now claiming. 'What does Hunt want with the heart?' asked Byron. 'He'll only put it in a glass case and make sonnets to it'.

Nevertheless, work on the first edition of the journal was well underway and the first edition appeared in October. It sold well and made a profit of £400.00 which Hunt received nearly £300. 'The Vision of Judgement', still one of the great satires in the English language and a conclusive response to Southey, led the charge:

He had written praises of a Regicide;
He had written praises of all kings whatever;
He had written for republics far and wide,
And then against them bitterer than ever;
For pantisocracy he once had cried
Aloud, a scheme less moral than 'twas clever;
Then grew a hearty anti-Jacobin--
Had turn'd his coat--and would have turn'd his skin.

He had sung against all battles, and again
In their high praise and glory; he had call'd
Reviewing "the ungentle craft," and then
Become as base a critic as e'er crawl'd--
Fed, paid, and pamper'd by the very men
By whom his muse and morals had been maul'd:
He had written much blank verse, and blanker prose,
And more of both than anybody knows.

Though Southey must have regretted his words 'when he attacks me again let it be in rhyme' its impact was blunted by two factors. Byron's celebrity status was partially squandered as he had published it under a pseudonym referencing a Spanish poet and satirist, and secondly, the preface, which gave important context to his response to Southey, had not appeared. It seems to have been withheld from John Hunt either by John Murray or Byron's friend Douglas Kinnaird – the reader must have felt confused.

In the end *The Liberal* went into four issues, and though often regarded as a failure, scholars like Jane Stabler have made more positive assessments. With its cosmopolitan tone it challenged narrow nationalist attitudes; in political terms it was a welcome counterblast to Tory journals like the *Quarterly Review*, and in religious terms it promoted a relaxed pantheist worldview contrasting with the anxious Anglicanism of the political establishment. It was, in fact, helping to lay the ground for the greater extent of free expression that The Beatles could enjoy a hundred and fifty years later. In the event John Hunt was charged with blasphemous libel for publishing Byron's 'Vision', and in January 1824 was fined £100.

Despite Byron's pledge to 'stand in Shelley's place' Hunt had instinctively known that his lost friend was irreplaceable. And so it proved. The Shelleys and the Hunts thought Byron immensely wealthy, but the truth was more complex, and he was trying to economise at the same time as having to support his own household and that of the Hunts. This could not help but grate on both sides, with Hunt's demands for money – 'I must trouble you for another cool hundred of your crowns' – irritating Byron. In turn the way that his accountant Lega Zambelli grudgingly doled out the money grated on him. Hunt's wife Marianne did not help. When Byron was telling the pair how he was under fire for his morals she replied memorably 'It is the first time I ever heard of them'. Hunt not very tactfully passed on her comment that a recent sketch of Byron made him 'look like a great schoolboy, who had been given a plain bun instead of a plum one'.

Teresa wrote that 'If Byron appeared to be in good spirits, Hunt called him heartless; if he took a bath, a sybarite. If he tried to joke with him, he was guilty of the unsufferable liberties that a great nobleman will allow himself with a poor man. If he presented Hunt with numerous copyrights, with the sole intention of helping him, it could only be because he lacked an editor. If he was charitable, it was out of ostentation'. Byron had his own memorable quote: assisting Hunt, he wrote, was 'like pulling a drowning man out of a river who directly throws himself in again'. And so, in Genoa, relations deteriorated, just as they would deteriorate amongst the four members of The Beatles, with finance at the heart of their discord. In the end, when Byron left for Greece, he would set off without even saying goodbye to Hunt. It was a sad finale to his relationship with Hunt, which had begun in such admiration, and ended in complete indifference.

14

'Give Greece back to the Grecians'

Though musicians like Woody Guthrie, the Weavers and others had raised money for political or social purposes, it was George Harrison's Concert for Bangladesh in 1971 which showed how the newly powerful music industry could be leveraged for humanitarian causes. He created a model that Bob Geldof used later with the Band Aid and Live Aid events, melding rival and competing artists into a greater whole. 'Leave your ego at reception' was the motto for contributors, prompting a contemporary cartoonist to depict one participant asking 'Can I have a receipt please?'

The world of rock and pop may well eclipse, in so many ways, that of the poets of the 19th century, but it's fair to say that Byron's contribution to the Greek War of Independence overshadows modern rock stars' efforts for charity. His commitment helped to found a modern European state, and redraw the boundaries of a continent, with the Ottoman empire ejected from its 400-year long European foothold. What he drew on though, was the same charismatic influence that George Harrison also could use when organising the Bangladesh concert, enlisting popular sympathy through celebrity power.

It is as if a contemporary rock star headed into the heart of the war in Ukraine, convinced it should be free from an empire's grasp and putting all his or her resources at the service of the cause. And he was under no illusions as to what he faced: the might of the Ottoman empire and the brutality of its actions. On his first trip to the near East he had seen its power firsthand in the Topkapi palace in

Istanbul, when he had accompanied a British government delegation making a diplomatic visit to the Sultan. The massacre on the Greek island of Chios in 1821, when virtually the whole island's population had been enslaved or put to the sword, was an example of how Ottoman troops could behave, and the beheading of Ali Pasha, the Albanian warlord who he had visited in his mountain stronghold, and who had rebelled against the Ottomans, was a recent demonstration of what he personally could face.

Known as the poet of passion *par excellence* Byron went against type in many ways with his Greek expedition. He had written: 'There is no such thing as a life of passion any more than a continuous earthquake, or an eternal fever. Besides, who would ever shave themselves in such a state?' In Genoa he had made meticulous preparations for the journey, aided by Pietro, Teresa's brother, and when he reached Cephalonia, under a British mandate, he told the missionary doctor James Kennedy that though 'everyone expects me to rush into Greece and die gloriously on the battlefield I must be cautious, I must put my energies to the best possible use'.

That he was right was shown by Trelawny who had accompanied him thus far but now went on by himself into Greece, professing himself tired of what he saw as Byron's procrastinations and dawdling. He made a disastrous alignment with a picturesque but self-serving warlord, Odysseus Androutsos, who was noted for his 'cruelty, bravery, guile and cupidity' and who was later executed by the Greeks for collaborating with the Ottomans. Trelawny's expedition came to an ignominious end when he was shot, wounded and shipped back to England in a British corvette.

Soon after arriving in Cephalonia Byron wrote to his friend Hobhouse, a founder member of the London Greek Committee: 'Great divisions and difficulties exist – and several foreigners have come away in great disgust as usual – it is at present my intention to remain here or there as long as I see a prospect of advantage to the cause, but I must not conceal from you and the Committee that the Greeks appear in more danger from their own divisions than from the attacks of the enemy'. Though respecting the bravery of the different Greek chieftains who were involved in the battle, he saw clearly into their limited factional ambitions, and had been firm with their representatives in Cephalonia, who wished to lure him and his money to their particular campaigns. 'To each of these I replied that I had not come to join a faction, but a nation'.

'I think it a thousand pities that he did not remain in Cephalonia' wrote the redoubtable Byron scholar (and fashion historian) Doris Langley Moore. 'He could still have exercised considerable influence … and we should have had several more cantos of our greatest comic epic'. But seeing that the Provisional Government of Western Greece, based in Missolonghi, had a national rather than a sectarian vision, and was led by Prince Mavrocordato who had been on good terms with the Shelleys in Pisa (Shelley had dedicated 'Hellas' to him and Mavrocordato, in the Casa Aulla overlooking the river Arno, had given Greek lessons to Mary), he eventually set off to offer his support.

On arrival he raised a brigade from the refugee Albanian Suliote warriors who had been driven from their mountain homes, paid for the restoration of the town's defences, provided funds to the Provisional Government, backed an application for a loan from London, and began making plans for military campaigns. His position as a palpably disinterested supporter of the Greeks gave him unique purchase in the effort to unite the disparate factions, and he struck exactly the right note as a foreign supporter of a national struggle. 'I am here to assist the Greeks in their own way, and on their own terms' he said.

In Missolonghi itself the situation could be tense: 'Between Suliote chiefs, German barons, English volunteers, and adventurers of all nations, we are likely to form as goodly an allied army as ever quarrelled under the same banner' he wrote. But on the larger level there was good news: the £800,000 loan from London, raised from private money and encouraged by Byron's presence in Greece, had been approved. This, some argue, was a decisive factor in shifting the balance of power decisively to the 'modernisers' like Mavrocordato.

Earlier, while on an expedition from Cephalonia, Byron had suffered a severe attack that must have been related to stress. While being welcomed to a monastery for a night's rest he suffered convulsions, abused the abbot who was giving a welcoming speech, (calling him a 'pestilential madman') and then trashed his room 'uttering desperate cries for relief from this hell'. For Doris Langley Moore this showed that he was 'unfit in health for the mission he had embarked on', but no one would tell him this to his face. Now, in Missolonghi, with the stress of the situation and a constitution weakened by a poor diet, together with his doctors' insistence on bleeding him after he had become feverish, Byron lay in his room realising that 'his hour had come'. As William Parry, a volunteer artilleryman who had become his confidant wrote: 'I have never before felt, as I felt that evening. There was the gifted Lord Byron, who had been the object of universal attention, who had, as a youth, been intoxicated with the idolatry of men and the more flattering love of women, gradually expiring, almost forsaken, and certainly without the consolation of breathing out his last sigh in the arms of some dear friend. His habitation was weathertight, but that was nearly all the comfort his deplorable room afforded him'.

'I had sense of deep sorrow to see him thus perishing, far from his home, far from all the comforts due to his rank and situation, far too from every fond and affectionate heart. The sirocco blew, and the rain fell with tropical violence'.

Back in Genoa Byron had told Lady Blessington of a childhood encounter with a fortune teller who had told him: 'Beware your 37th year, my young Lord, Beware!' Her prophecy turned out to be accurate – a mere three months after his 36th birthday he passed away in Missolonghi.

The Greek cannons sounded dolefully across the lagoon – when the Turks heard why they were firing they shot off their muskets in celebration. The Sultan was no doubt pleased; he had recently held a full session of his court where Byron had been pronounced an 'enemy of the Porte'. Greece was inconsolable: a period of mourning was announced in Missolonghi and during Easter week a funeral oration was delivered which stated: 'Had Byron remained at home he might with his financial assistance alone have saved Greece, but this was not sufficient. He was one destined by nature to uphold the rights of man whenever he saw them trampled on, one who knew not only what man is, but what he ought to be, and what he may be'.

When news of Byron's death reached his homeland it 'came upon London like an earthquake', according to the writer Allan Cunningham writing in the *London Magazine*. Jane Welsh, later to marry Thomas Carlyle, wrote to her future husband: 'Byron is dead. Byron is dead! I was told it all at once in a roomful of people. My God, if they had said that the sun or the moon had gone out of the heavens, it could not have struck me with the idea of a more awful and dreary blank in the creation'. Carlyle himself wrote that Byron was 'the noblest spirit in Europe'.

The 14-year-old Alfred Tennyson walked out of his house in Somersby in Lincolnshire and wrote 'Byron is dead' upon a rock as if he had to see it there to believe it. The 18-year-old Elizabeth Barrett Browning sat down and wrote her 'Stanzas on the death of Lord Byron', noting his sacrifice for Greece – 'That generous heart whose genius thrilled divine/Hath spent its last most glorious throb for thee', but adding that 'my soul shall find/A language in these tears'.

'No one could remember', another contemporary commentator wrote, 'the death of a poet having such an impact', and John Clare, in London's Tottenham Court Road as his funeral procession set out for Hucknall Torkard in Nottinghamshire, remembered how the crowd 'moved in saddened silence', also noting how a young girl, 'dark and beautiful', whispered 'poor Lord Byron' as the hearse and the mourning coaches (many of them empty) set off. London's great families had sent them, but not wanting to be associated with Byron, his life or his politics, had decided not to attend in person. The contrast between the girl's sigh and the spineless aristocrats led Clare to conclude that it 'was better to be loved by the common people than flattered by the great', adding that 'The common people felt his merits and his power and the common people of a country are the best feelings of a prophesy of futurity'.

Which were sentiments that could equally apply, just over 150 years later, to the feelings produced by the news of John Lennon's murder in New York. As the Encyclopaedia Britannica said of Byron, his 'poetry and personality had captured the imagination of Europe', except in John Lennon's case he had become even more of a worldwide icon. His involvement in the larger-than-life story of The Beatles, his complex personality, the way that he had become part of people's lives, the sense of waste and the loss of someone who could somehow reflect and clarify, the additional sense that someone who despite his admitted personal failings still generated a sense of moral direction – all these were qualities that he could be seen as sharing with Byron. Their early deaths had similar effects among their admirers.

Shelley had described a contented time in his and Mary's life which matched John Lennon's last years in the Dakota:

> Now has descended a serener hour...
> And from thy side two gentle babes are born
> To fill our home with smiles, and thus are we
> Most fortunate beneath life's beaming morn;
> And these delights, and thou, have been to me
> The parents of the Song I consecrate to thee.

All the more poignant then, that his murder should coincide with such a state of affairs, which ironically also pointed to a spiritual realignment with his long-time friend, partner and rival Paul. Having scorned the domesticity of his 1971 album 'Ram' whose then unfashionable watchwords were

'Home, Family, Love', Lennon had just released 'Double Fantasy' whose values were identical.

Almost everyone has their specific memory of hearing of John Lennon's death: in my own case I was in London on the morning that news that John Lennon had been murdered in New York came through. On the bus to work, not having heard the morning broadcasts, I felt from somewhere a feeling of immense sadness and remember thinking – 'that's funny, where did that come from?' I was told by a workmate, mid-morning, of what had happened, rushed out to get a paper at lunchtime, and stared disbelievingly at its headline 'JOHN LENNON SHOT DEAD' and its equally unbelievable subtitle 'Smiling gunman fires five bullets into ex-Beatle'. At the end of the day there was total silence on the bus journey home, and in the evening the news broadcasters had all dressed in black.

There are of course plenty of videos and images online testifying to the shock of people across America, in Liverpool and across Britain, in India, the rest of Asia and all the countries, English-speaking or not, which The Beatles had touched during their seven year public career. Type 'Death of John Lennon' into a search engine and you will encounter a deep pool of sadness and incomprehension that will enable you to feel yourself back into the response in 1824 to the news of Byron's death: 'no one could remember the death of a poet having such an impact', 'it felt as if I had lost a brother'.

PART THREE

1824-2024:
The Comets' Fiery Tails

15

'The long and winding road'

One of the key differences between the Younger Romantics and The Beatles, as noted, was their different trajectories of fame. The Beatles achieved fame together and with a bang; back in the 1820s Byron had been the one with the overarching media and popular presence. Yet over time Keats and Shelley would come to match Byron in terms of popular acclaim: recognition built as new editions, anthologies and biographies slowly but steadily appeared. Together with Byron they were on their way, with Leigh Hunt in tow, to be, eventually, grouped together, with a name of their own: 'The Younger Romantics'.

Keats had died on 23rd February 1821. In a sequence of events traced by Romantics scholar Nicholas Roe, four days later Joseph Severn wrote with the news to Keats's friend Charles Brown in Hampstead; it was eighteen days before the letter arrived one Saturday evening. The following morning 'He went next door at Wentworth Place and he told Fanny Brawne, that her fiancé had died'. Brown then wrote a series of letters, including one to Keats's publisher John Taylor asking him to place a notice in the London newspapers. On March 22nd a brief announcement appeared in the Morning Chronicle: "At Rome, on 23 February, of a decline, John Keats, the Poet, aged 25."

Roe shows that the announcement was picked up by 34 London newspapers as well as provincial papers from Bristol to Inverness, and argues that: 'Those announcements amount to a kind of seedbed, planted in popular consciousness and public awareness, that a poet named John Keats had existed and that he had died at Rome, aged 25. From this seedbed, Keats's reputation was primed and poised to grow'.

Though most of Shelley's work at the time of his death was unpublished, and what had been published had rarely sold well, his notoriety as a high-profile atheist and perceived advocate of free love meant that his death caused a flurry of controversy in the British press. When Hunt announced his death in *The Examiner* a leading Tory journal, the *Courier*, responded almost exultantly: 'Shelley, the writer of some infidel poetry, has been drowned: now he knows whether there is a God or no'. The populist high Tory magazine *John Bull* joined in with 'Mr Byshe (sic) Shelley, the author of that abominable and blasphemous book called Queen Mab, was lately drowned in a storm somewhere in the Mediterranean. His object in visiting that part of the world, it was stated, was to coalesce with some others of his opinions to *write down* Christianity. The visitation is, therefore, striking; and the termination of his life (considering his creed) not more awful than *surprising*'.

But *John Bull* had its own opponent, *The Real John Bull*, who, as Sylva Norman noted, 'was shocked by the "religious bigotry and party spirit" that could lead "the infamous *John Bull*" to utter "a demoniac yell of joy at the poet's drowning".

Norman summarised the ensuing battle: '*John Bull* railed at the *Chronicle* at huge length, the *Chronicle* censured The *Courier*, the *British Luminary* parodied *John Bull*, the *Republica* reprinted the *Luminary*, and finally the Leigh Hunt letter reappeared in the Paris *Monthly Review* for August….'

What was missing though was, as noted, a rounded understanding of Shelley's poetic achievement. It was Mary Shelley who stepped in to rectify the situation. As Sara Martín Alegre puts it: 'his writings would not have survived without Mary's editorial intervention and her determination to make them be known'. Anna Mercer, a leading analyst of Shelley and Mary's collaborative literary relationship adds: 'Within a few weeks of PBS's death MWS had made plans to support herself through her own compositions and by publishing PBS's poetry and editing his manuscripts'.

Mary's contribution was profound and exacting. Even though Shelley's manuscripts are often hugely difficult to decipher, in the end she only made one significant mistake in terms of the text, misreading 'mutiny' as 'mystery' in the line 'their might could not repress the mutiny within' in his final unfinished poem 'The Triumph of Life'. She was familiar with much of his work and as Charles Robinson puts it:

'The Shelleys left a long history of their shared activities as creative artists. They transcribed and they edited each other's works; they encouraged each other to undertake or to modify major works; and they even collaborated in the publication of 'History of a Six Week's Tour' at a time when 'Frankenstein' was being readied for the press'.

During his lifetime Mary kept a fair copy ledger of Shelley's works from which copies could be made for publication, and provided critical feedback, as Shelley's introduction to 'The Witch of Atlas' showed:

To Mary (On Her Objecting to the Following Poem, Upon the Score of its Containing No Human Interest)

How, my dear Mary, -- are you critic-bitten
(For vipers kill, though dead) by some review,
That you condemn these verses I have written,
Because they tell no story, false or true?
What, though no mice are caught by a young kitten
May it not leap and play as grown cats do,
Till its claws come? Prithee, for this one time,
Content thee with a visionary rhyme.

Their relationship, Mercer notes, is 'often misrepresented as that of a patriarchal husband exerting intellectual dominance over his wife'; it looks more like a creative relationship comparable to that of John Lennon and Yoko Ono, including a widow's calling to keep her husband's work alive after his death.

And so she began working on an edition of Shelley's collected poems, 'Posthumous Poems', which, in 1824, was published in an edition of 500 by John Hunt. She had written prophetically that 'the world will surely one day feel what it lost when this bright child of song deserted her', but these sentiments were not shared by Shelley's father Sir Timothy Shelley. Still appalled at the supposed disgrace his son had brought on the family name ('Sir T. writhes under the fame of his incomparable son' wrote Mary), he threatened to withdraw the allowance she depended on for her son Percy

Florence unless it was withdrawn. And so it went out of print, but that was not the end of the story.

For Shelley's 'Queen Mab', first printed by Shelley in a private edition of 250 in 1813, had been first pirated in 1820 and during the following decade would be reprinted again and again. 'Rock 'n' roll is naughty' Tina Turner once said, but over time that naughtiness becomes normalised into the social flow and its impact is forgotten. There are plenty of Beatles songs with sly references to drugs and sex that shocked sensibilities at the time, but now hardly raise an eyebrow. Similarly, the shock value of the now classic poems of Shelley and Byron is difficult to grasp today.

'Queen Mab' was the naughtiest thing on the market. Its pirating in 1820 was described by Shelley as 'a droll circumstance', and he was no doubt pleased to be told by Hunt that it was 'selling like hot cakes on the Charing Cross Road'. So even if Mary's beautiful edition 'Posthumous Poems' had been withdrawn, as William St Clair shows, 'the revolutionary Queen Mab was sold cheaply (enough) for dissemination among the populace'... 'It enjoyed a large sale, and was never out of print'. Paul Foot in 'Red Shelley' adds more detail about its publication history, noting that the original publisher of the pirated edition William Clarke was threatened by the 'Society for the Suppression of Vice' and withdrew it, but that it was then reprinted by the fearless Richard Carlile, and continued on its way with up to 30 editions appearing in the 1820s. As Richard Holmes put it, 'Shelley's name was assured currency in the working movement for the next twenty years'. Hunt's publication of 'The Mask of Anarchy' in 1832 only added to his credibility.

Byron of course was widely read, with his death spurring increased interest in his life and work. As noted, memoirs and biographies were widely available, and 'Don Juan', denied copyright because of its 'injurious' nature, circulated both in the cheap editions produced by John Hunt and pirated editions that could not be suppressed. 'In consequence, St Clair concludes that in its first twenty years '*Don Juan* was read by more people than any previous work of English literature'. Byron was influential in the USA as well, with the *Harvard Gazette* noting that 'nearly 100 editions of Byron's works were published in America during his lifetime and many more afterward'.

The stream of admiring, uncritical or openly gushing Byron books led one publisher to spot a gap in the market. There must be room for a 'knocking job' reasoned Henry Colburn, and he knew just the right person to approach. It was Leigh Hunt of course, no doubt full of information about the noble Lord and his personal life gleaned from the now defunct '*Liberal*' project. In 1825 Hunt was marooned in Florence, hardly surviving on the writing assignments that came his way. 'The dinner of the family is one dish of the cheapest kind', wrote Keats's friend Charles Brown. 'They sit over a shivering fire during the bitter cold of an Italian winter'. So when Colburn offered a £200 advance for a suitably critical addition to the flood of Byron books Hunt jumped at the chance. He paid eighty-two guineas for transport to England in a horse-drawn carriage, and was back in London in October. 'Lord Byron and Some of his Contemporaries' duly appeared two years later, preceded by extracts in magazines which expertly primed the market.

While Colburn did very well financially out of the book, friends of Byron were appalled, and Hunt's charges against Byron, that he was mean and avaricious, envious of others' achievements, did not know 'what real love is', was superstitious, not as brave as portrayed by others, and so on, drew down a storm of criticism on his head. It was a 'miserable book by a miserable man', full of 'filthy gossip' and 'ingratitude' and indeed has long been seen as a stain on Hunt's career. However, the passages on Shelley and Keats continued his record of promoting and defending them. In addition to lauding Shelley, he described Keats as 'A man of genius … one of those who are too genuine and too original to be properly appreciated at first, but whose time for applause will infallibly arrive'. In a similar vein, he had written in his 'Sonnet to Percy Shelley':

Yes, wild ocean's wave
Hath o'er thee rolled. But while within the grave
Thou sleepst, let me in the love of thy pure worth
One thing foretell, that thy great fame shall be
Progressive as Time's flood, eternal as the sea!

He was right: Mary Shelley's role in editing and publishing his manuscripts finally bore fruit in 1839, when her four volume collection of Shelley's poems was published. 'Obstacles have long existed to my presenting the public with a perfect edition of Shelley's poems' her introduction began – at last 19th century readers were presented with something approaching the full spectrum of a great poet's output. It was supplemented by an edition of selected essays, letters and translations which Mary published in the same year.

At this point Keats seems still to have been relatively neglected. Though his work had been included in the Parisian publisher Galignani's 1829 edition (which Wordsworth possessed), Stanley Plumly, the author of 'Posthumous Keats', notes that in 1845 his publisher John Taylor 'sold the copyright to the poems and unpublished manuscripts for next to nothing, underscoring the fact that the poet's work was effectively out of print in England'. However, he did have his admirers, one of whom, Richard Monkton Milnes, part of a literary group which included Tennyson, rescued him from neglect and a generally unfavourable estimate of his work in 1848 through the two volume 'Life, Letters and Literary Remains of John Keats'.

His biography would help to give Keats an entry into the visual arts, because when it was read by Dante Gabriel Rossetti it created an important link with the Pre-Raphaelite painters – and the historic Italian artists who were the group's chief source of inspiration. Rossetti was excited to find that Keats had specifically referenced them, and in 1848 wrote to his brother William (who later became an important advocate for, and editor of Shelley's work):

'I have not yet had time to get quite through the first volume of Keats, which is exceedingly interesting. He seems to have been a glorious fellow, and says in one place (to my great delight) that, having just looked over a folio of the first and second schools of Italian painting, he has come to the conclusion that the early men surpassed even Raphael himself!'

So Keats came to the attention of the Pre-Raphaelites, who saw him as a kindred spirit and a poet whose work could translate into the lush imagery they favoured. Their depictions of scenes from Keats's work

('The Eve of St Agnes', 'Isabella; or, The Pot of Basil', 'La Belle Dame Sans Merci') would give him a new dimension in the public sphere. Byron of course, was already well represented through paintings of his work, including 'Lord Byron's dream' (1827) by Charles Eastlake and John Martin's 'Manfred on the Jungfrau' (1837).

In 1857, across continents and in the land where the East India Company had assumed greater and greater powers, the event known variously as the Indian Mutiny, the Sepoy Mutiny, the Great Rebellion, the Indian Insurrection, or the First War of Independence took place, to the shock and surprise of the British ruling class. If they had read their Byron though, they might not have been caught unawares. In his poem 'The Curse of Minerva', written in Athens as sculptures from the Parthenon were being removed by Lord Elgin, he drew wider lessons about what he had called 'this mania for collecting colonies' and referred to India in an excoriating, prophetic stanza:

> Look to the East, where Ganges' swarthy race
>   Shall shake your tyrant empire to its base;
> Lo! there Rebellion rears her ghastly head,
>   And glares the Nemesis of native dead;
>   Till Indus rolls a deep purpureal flood,
> And claims his long arrear of northern blood.
> So may ye perish!—Pallas, when she gave
> Your free-born rights, forbade ye to enslave.

A reminder of Byron's continuing anti-imperialistic influence, it bears out the Slapp Happy song 'The Unborn Byron', which concludes with the embryonic poet maintaining that his life of 'unbuttoned liberty' will be remembered by 'the unborn'.

Two years later the last link with the young poets who had tried to establish a creative centre of power in Pisa was broken. Leigh Hunt, now an 'old man with snowy hair, … brilliant eyes' and 'a fascinating grace of manner', finally died. 'So gentle was the final approach' his son Thornton wrote, 'that he scarcely recognised it to the last, and then it came without terrors'. In his final days he had been revising his 'Autobiography of Leigh Hunt', which now featured a more charitable assessment of Byron as well as his reminiscences of Keats and Shelley. As a survivor of a period of high octane creativity he can be compared to a survivor of the 1960s, befriending and championing new writers and artists but with the feeling perhaps, that whatever their merits, they were 'dismal candles' compared to the poetic luminaries he had consorted with.

The 1860s also saw a cultural development worth noting as a critical marker in the century and a half journey between Romanticism and The Beatles. The nonsense poetry pioneered by Edward Lear and the prototype surrealism introduced in 'Alice in Wonderland' by Lewis Carroll brought a whole new dimension to English-speaking culture. 'Alice in Wonderland', John Lennon would always say, was one of the books that 'really opened my whole being', and the influence of Lear and Carroll can be seen in the Spike Milligan-written 'Goon Show', a favourite of the young John Lennon, and would ultimately emerge in songs like 'I Am The Walrus', 'Glass Onion', 'Yellow Submarine' and 'Come Together'. It is difficult, if not impossible, to find the surrealist sensibility that pervades many Beatles songs anywhere in Romantic literature.

At the end of the following decade a piece of poetry, 'Dover Beach' by Matthew Arnold would be published. It marked a tipping point between the European societies which had regarded Shelley's atheistic declarations with horror and Lennon's 'more popular than Jesus' comment with comparative indifference. In his poem, published in 1867, Matthew Arnold referred to the 'melancholy, long withdrawing roar' of the 'Sea of Faith'. New geological understandings and evolutionary theory were undermining literal Biblically-based beliefs, and the monopolistic power of the Anglican Church was waning. The passage of time saw a further erosion of faith, with the result that mainstream European opinion was little disturbed by Lennon's 'more popular than Jesus' comment in the mid-1960s. However, American Bible Belt religiosity had been relatively unaffected by such transformations, hence the strong reactions to his remark.

By the 1870s Keats, Shelley and Byron were now also finding their way into a range of new media. As set out in Tom Mole's 'What the Victorians made of Romanticism', there now also appeared, in addition to the contribution of the Pre-Raphaelites, 'illustrated books, anthologies, statues, postcards and memorial plaques'. He notes that these new gave the Romantics new momentum, and synchronised them with ongoing cultural developments.

Though Tom Mole's analysis of the Victorian Shelley anthologies reveals how the lyrical and the descriptive were selected rather than the politically contentious, he is relatively charitable about these omissions. Even if they continued the practice of censoring Shelley's work they could create an interest that might lead the reader back to the original. There was now a demand for a biography of the poet, satisfied by Edward Dowden's Life in 1886. Produced with the approval and assistance of the

Shelley family (Shelley's son Sir Percy Florence Shelley and Lady Jane Shelley) it had to skirt the various aspects of the poet's life that would not sit well in the Victorian era. However, it was still influential: Walt Whitman was one of its readers and later became a firm friend of Dowden, who in turn became a champion of his work.

The publication of Keats's letters to Fanny Brawne in 1878 had raised his profile, even if they attracted much criticism. As Małgorzata Łuczyńska-Hołdys puts it, 'Seen from the vantage point of the Victorian sensibility, the letters express first of all a 'vulgar excess' … and secondly, they mark Keats as a sensuous, and therefore effeminate poet who allows himself to be flooded by emotions and passion'. 'After the publication of the letters in 1878', she concludes, 'the perception of Keats as "feminine" became standard during the Victorian era'.

By the 1870s therefore, fifty years after Keats, Shelley and Byron had passed into history, they had achieved a parity of recognition and could be seen as a distinctive group, collected together under the name The Younger Romantics. Which invites the question: what is the position now with The Beatles, at time of writing also fifty years on from their split?

Like the Romantics, The Beatles are also moving into new media, and also are subject to shifting perceptions. The release of Peter Jackson's 7-hour Beatles documentary 'Get Back' in 2021 not only transformed the picture of The Beatles given in the previous shorter film 'Let it Be' but also has led to a significant shift in attitudes to Paul McCartney. Previously under attack for being bossy, breaking up The Beatles (allegedly), and for producing music which John Lennon described as 'musak to my ears', he appeared in the film in a very different light, relaxed about John Lennon's new relationship with Yoko Ono, trying to keep the band together and on the verge of tears when its future seemed to be in jeopardy. He was also keen to take on 'The Man' ('wouldn't it be great if we all got arrested?') and oozed musicality with his conjuring up of 'Get Back' in the studio, providing them with a song which brought the best out of each of them. McCartney himself found Jackson's film had a therapeutic effect on his memories: 'I loved it' he said, 'I really forgave myself when I saw that'.

With the development of streaming there has also come the opportunity to assess their popularity – and George Harrison, the Keatsian late developer, tops the 2022 Spotify list with 825 million streams.

1. 'Here Comes The Sun' – 825m
2. 'Come Together' – 515m
3. 'Let It Be' – 466m
4. 'Hey Jude' – 442m
5. 'Yesterday' – 419m
6. 'Twist and Shout' – 300m
7. 'Blackbird' – 287m
8. 'In My Life' – 230m
9. 'Something' – 204m
10. 'Help!' – 224m

John Lennon would undoubtedly be pleased that 'Come Together' leads Paul's songs, but Paul can take comfort from his overall representation with the most songs included – and the most streams overall.

An equivalent inventory made at the equivalent date of 1874 would undoubtedly show Lord Byron leading in the stakes for 'individual reads'. He was well known not just in Continental European countries, especially France, Poland and Russia, but had also made his way across the Atlantic, where 'after his death, in both North and South America, Byron became the symbolic icon of British Romanticism and the embodiment of modernity'. He also, as noted by Christine Kenyon Jones, made 'a notable cultural contribution to the movement for the abolition of transatlantic slavery', highlighting Matt Sandler's demonstration that an 'extraordinary array' of African-American writers, including Frederick Douglass, made widespread use of lines from Canto II of 'Childe Harold':

> Hereditary bondsmen! Know ye not
> Who would be free themselves must first strike the blow?

John Keats would probably be in the second position with his narrative poems like 'Isabella; or, The Pot of Basil' chiming with the Victorian readership. Shelley would probably be lower down the order and with slightly surprising poems like 'A Vision of the Sea' performing strongly (due to the Victorian fascination with shipwrecks). Leigh Hunt would also make an appearance with poems like 'Jenny Kissed Me' registering strongly.

If Shelley was indeed under-performing in terms of his readers he was still having a crucial social influence by encouraging the ongoing pressure for democratic change. He can be seen as helping to nurture the self-education movement, when even the impoverished, in their cottages, can build a new world for themselves:

Science, Poetry and Thought
Are thy lamps, they make the lot
Of a dweller in a cot, so serene
They curse it not

In political terms, as Mary wrote in 1839: 'His influence over mankind, though slow in growth, is fast augmenting; and, in the ameliorations that have taken place in the political state of his country, we may trace in part the operation of his arduous struggles'.

She was right: Paul Foot's 'Red Shelley' describes his impact on the Chartist movement which had peaked in the 1850s, and which, though failing in its initial aim had created the conditions for the widening of the franchise in 1867 and 1884.

He also charts the influence of Shelley's feminist verses –

'Woman and Man, in confidence and love, equal and free', from 'Queen Mab';

'Can Man be Free if Woman be a slave?' from 'The Revolt of Islam'; and

'Women, frank and beautiful and kind,
Speaking the wisdom once they could not think,
Looking emotions once they feared to feel,
And changed to all which once they dared not be'

from 'Prometheus Unbound' on the growing movement campaigning for womens' rights including the right to vote. Not only were key 19th century 'influencers' inspired by Shelley, but suffragette campaigners from 1906 to 1914 saw him as a supportive voice. As well as Millicent Fawcett, Foot states that he was a favourite of the Pankhurst family, Emmeline and her daughters Sylvia and Christobel. At the same time, across the Atlantic, the New York trade unionist Pauline Newman was inspired by Shelley to fight for better working conditions and for gender equality within trades unions too.

In many ways the Chartists and the Suffragettes were the truest readers of Shelley, but there was always a strong contingent of those who could see Shelley's talents but deplored his irreligion and radicalism. The anthologies had been one response: 'This volume leaves out *all* Shelley's contentious poems' one compiler proudly declared, and the Catholic mystic poet Francis Thompson wrote an influential essay in 1910 which located him firmly in the world of whimsy. Commenting on his shorter lyrics for example he wrote: 'He plays truant from earth, slips through the wicket of fancy into heaven's meadow, and goes gathering stars'. 'His worshippers have made such a fool of Shelley that we dare not speak of him' one social activist wrote.

However, Shelley had an admirer in the person of the war poet Wilfred Owen, described by Dominic Hibberd as 'the last great heir to the Romantics'. Shelley's conception of the social role of the poet would sustain Owen in the trenches (in his last weeks he was 'reading plenty of Shelley'), but it was Keats rather than Shelley whose influence can be traced in what Hibberd described as Owen's 'last and best war poem', 'Spring Offensive'.

The very situation of 'Spring Offensive' recalls 'To Autumn': the scene that Keats conjured up in his poem, the Hampshire landscape around Winchester, is also trembling on the brink of destruction. Winter will sweep in and, we all know, put an end to the warm tranquil landscape Keats was describing. It was poised, like the soldiers in 'Spring Offensive' on the brink of change.

Owen's poem begins with an image of ease: having walked up a long valley some of the soldiers 'carelessly sleep', with the wording echoing Keats's image of Autumn, 'on a half-reaped furrow sound asleep'. They march through the 'warm field' with its echo of Keats's bees who 'think warm days will never cease', and Owen observes that 'the buttercup had blessed with gold their slow boots coming up', recalling Keats's line 'conspiring with him how to load and bless'.

Now, on the ridge, the soldiers who did not sleep looked back on the valley and saw 'the long grass swirled by the May breeze': grass 'murmurous with wasp and midge' like Keats's 'wailful choir' where 'the small gnats mourn'. Keats's Autumn had been 'Drowsed with the fume of poppies' while asleep in the field, or sitting patiently by a cider-press, where 'Thou watchest the last oozings hours by hours'. For Owen's soldiers, though 'the summer oozed though their veins/Like an injected drug for their bodies' pains', they know this cannot last. 'Sharp on their souls hung the imminent line of grass': the ridge over which they would have to make their attack and leave their temporary haven of warm restfulness beckons ominously.

They remained there
Till like a cold gust thrills the little word

At which each body and its soul begird
And tighten them for battle…

Soon they topped the hill, and raced together
Over an open stretch of herb and heather
Exposed. And instantly the whole sky burned
With fury against them; earth set sudden cups
In thousands for their blood…

'A beaker full of the warm South, with beaded bubbles winking at the brim'; just short of a century after his death Keats's technique of 'poetic concentration', once deployed to convey the beauty and joy of wine, now re-emerged in the ghastly killing fields of World War One: 'earth set sudden cups/In thousands for their blood'. In the midst of all that horror, unremarked but lasting, the Younger Romantics were still a presence to be felt.

16
'The Long and Winding Road' II

Wilfred Owen's interest in Keats had been stimulated and strengthened by late Victorian developments in the publishing and memorializing of Keats and his work. The mid-century biography by Richard Monkton Milnes had played a critical role in getting the poet established, the edition of Keats's passionate letters to Fanny Brawne had created interest and controversy, the Keats-Shelley Association had been founded in 1903 with the rooms on the Spanish steps in Rome being purchased and opened as a memorial in 1906, and a full biography by Sidney Colvin had appeared in 1907.

The sensuality and rich versifying of his work, which had been alien to many readers in his own time, had now been assimilated and no longer seemed unacceptable; the scale of his achievement was now acknowledged. When Colvin approached Thomas Hardy to try to work out exactly where the poet had put ashore in England for the last time, Hardy suggested it had could have been Lulworth Cove in Dorset; the scenery seemed to accord with diary descriptions by Keats's companion Joseph Severn. The exchange prompted Hardy to write his moving poem to Keats, 'At Lulworth Cove a Century Back':

Had I but lived a hundred years ago
I might have gone, as I have gone this year,
By Warmwell Cross on to a Cove I know,
And Time have placed his finger on me there:

'You see that man?' — I might have looked, and said,
'O yes: I see him. One that boat has brought
Which dropped down Channel round Saint Alban's Head.
So commonplace a youth calls not my thought.'

'You see that man?' — 'Why yes; I told you; yes:
Of an idling town-sort; thin; hair brown in hue;
And as the evening light scants less and less
He looks up at a star, as many do.'

'You see that man?' — 'Nay, leave me!' then I plead,
'I have fifteen miles to vamp across the lea,
And it grows dark, and I am weary-kneed:
I have said the third time; yes, that man I see!'

'Good. That man goes to Rome — to death, despair;
And no one notes him now but you and I:
A hundred years, and the world will follow him there,
And bend with reverence where his ashes lie.'

So by 1920 Keats's reputation seems relatively secure; in the same year, in the Warton lecture on English poetry, the Scottish critic and academic H.J.C. Grierson referred to the vicissitudes Byron's literary reputation had undergone but noted his continuing value: 'In the house of poetry there are many mansions; and if Byron has been over-estimated and underestimated, English poetry would be greatly the poorer without his passionate, humorous, in all its register, essentially human voice'.

Shelley, however, was still subject to wild swings in critical judgements. The emasculated Victorian view of Shelley as set out by Matthew Arnold, who had labelled him a 'beautiful and ineffectual angel, beating in the void his luminous wings in vain' had been influential. In the first half of the 20th century the poet T.S. Eliot and the critic F.R. Leavis launched powerful attacks on him – or what they thought was him.

As the Scarriet cultural blog, under the heading 'Rejecting Shelley, did the Moderns suppress not only beautiful poetry, but love itself?', puts it:

'The strange assault on Shelley by the Modernists is perhaps best exemplified by T.S. Eliot's 1932 Norton Lecture at Harvard; Eliot happily escaped England *and his wife* to tour and visit the United States in a triumphant homecoming. The ire and visceral hatred for both Shelley's "ideas" and his "poetry" expressed by Eliot at Harvard was profound: Old Possum admitted that he literally could not stomach the "adolescent" Shelley. Eliot's attack took the same form as another sexless-American-author-turned-Brit's attack: on Poe—by Henry James'.

And Morris Dickstein summed up Leavis's approach to Shelley: 'Leavis finds Shelley's writing sentimental, vague, incoherent—the epitome of a certain kind of lush and breathless romanticism in which self-indulgence and effusiveness fill the place of precise thought, diction and imagery'.

As Foot noted, Leavis was so influential that readers dismissed Shelley without even reading him, and due to him and the attitudes of orthodox Leftists, Shelley was marginalised in the '1950s and 1960s almost as effectively as he had been when he was alive'.

However, across the Atlantic a trio of American scholars had been publishing game-changing contributions to the understanding of Shelley in the form of Newman Ivey White's massive biography, F.L. Jones's Letters, and Kenneth Neil Cameron's politically sympathetic studies. Suddenly a Shelley emerged who spoke compellingly to the post-1960s generations, and further publications – particularly Richard Holmes's 'Shelley: The Pursuit' (1974) and Paul Foot's 'Red Shelley' (1981) – popularised a new, more complex Shelley. Scholars showed that the allegedly lazy imagery that Leavis had complained about was nothing of the sort. No longer would the cock-eyed Victorian Shelley do – Arnold's 'ineffectual angel' now appeared to be precisely the opposite, a poet whose work had directly contributed to democratic advances. The poet 'whose idea of love was two angels holding hands' turned out to be a very modern exponent of women's rights and gender equality.

Then, in the 1990s, the Modernists themselves were subject to a devastating critique. According to the 2023 Amazon blurb, John Carey's 'The Intellectuals and the Masses' 'caused consternation throughout the artistic and academic establishments when it was first published in 1992'.

'Professor John Carey shows how early twentieth-century intellectuals imagined the 'masses' as semi-human swarms, drugged by popular newspapers and cinema, and ripe for extermination. Exposing the revulsion from common humanity in George Bernard Shaw, Ezra Pound, D. H. Lawrence, E. M. Forster, Virginia Woolf, H. G. Wells,

Aldous Huxley, and W. B. Yeats … he relates this to the cult of the Nietzschean Superman, which found its ultimate exponent in Hitler'.

The implication was that the real cause of the deep divide between the Modernists and Shelley was the poet's intrinsically democratic instincts, which had been so clearly demonstrated in 'The Mask of Anarchy'. As Mary Shelley had written: 'Shelley loved the People; and respected them as often more virtuous, as always more suffering, and therefore more deserving of sympathy, than the great. He believed that a clash between the two classes of society was inevitable, and he eagerly ranged himself on the people's side'. Far from seeing the 'masses' as 'semi-human swarms', Shelley emphasised their innate potential, which, he argued, was always capable of producing cultural and political excellence.

'The mass of capabilities remains at every period materially the same; the circumstances which awaken it to action perpetually change. If England were divided into forty republics, each equal in population and extent to Athens, there is no reason to suppose but that, under institutions not more perfect than those of Athens, each would produce philosophers and poets equal to those who (if we except Shakespeare) have never been surpassed'.

With diametrically opposite values, the Modernist movement arose at the same time as universal literacy amongst the British population was achieved, around 1900. Now the educated writers and artists, wishing to distinguish themselves from the masses, with their popular newspapers and magazines, vulgar theatre and musicals, began to develop forms of art with a peculiar egotism, that would emphasise the learning and stature of the artistic producer. They had lost their place as the only literate characters around; now they sought to reassert their superior status by producing works which the masses could not readily understand.

You could argue that T.S. Eliot's poem 'The Waste Land', first published in 1922, was an accurate reflection of the confused, fearful and fragmented situation after World War I. But John Carey's analysis, which describes how some sections of the poem continue to defy understanding, and argues that their 'difficulty' in fact amounts to 'unintelligibility', also rings true. As he says: 'Our normal word for things that cannot be understood is 'unintelligible', and in descriptions of high art, particularly high modernist art, this might be more accurate than 'difficult'.

Whatever the merits of modernist iconoclasm (and Carey will gladly concede that Eliot was 'a great phrasemaker'), its effect was to drive poetry further away from its popular audience. The human bond that Byron had enjoyed was broken; a vacuum had been created, and if you accept Shelley's explanation for the origins of poetry's appeal, you can see why the move away from poetry as a mass medium occurred.

This rupture would coincide with the growing influence of the recording industry, which was now bringing jazz, rhythm and blues and popular song to a wide audience. According to the American academic Robert Pattison, this fused with Romanticism to create the new form of rock 'n' roll. Black Southern music and the Romanticism made widely available through the education system (with a less pragmatic focus than elsewhere) provided the ideal breeding ground for rock. So, 'Romanticism lived on in the schoolroom as in the life of the South, and English was Elvis's favourite class in his Tennessee high school'. And the music that influenced Elvis came largely from the black population in his area, not just the gospel music at the church he attended with his family, but that of black blues-players in the area.

According to this understanding it was through Elvis Presley that the rhythmic power of African-American culture was fused with the poetic power of Romanticism, and poetry in a new form – backed by rhythm and blues – appeared. To the presumed horror of the Regency's cultural snobs the world of Keats, Leigh Hunt, Shelley and Byron, linked with the new, shockingly irrational force of rhythm and sensuality, had emphatically triumphed. A new reality had emerged: poetic expression was largely encountered through popular music. Which is the world we inhabit, with the technologies of the 1960s now looking laughably primitive, and with popular song ubiquitous, seeping into ever more areas.

Shelley's argument was that 'Poetry is ever allied with pleasure', and rhythm was a crucial part of its attraction. 'In the youth of the world, men dance and sing and imitate natural objects, observing in these actions, as in all others, a certain rhythm or order....' And, he continued, 'there is a certain order of rhythm ... from which the hearer and spectator receive an intenser and purer pleasure than from any other....' In other words, rhyme and rhythm are intrinsic to humanity – from nursery rhymes and football chants to limericks and epic poems, from Homer to hymns, from Beatles songs to hip hop, reggae and Rap – otherwise known as Rhythm and Poetry…

While it would be wrong to insist that all poetry must adhere to strict rhythmic guidelines, it could also be argued that abandoning the originating impulse behind poetry, as set out by Shelley, does have certain consequences. As Ayn Rand once memorably put it: 'You can ignore reality, but you can't ignore the consequences of ignoring reality'. In the case of poetry, those consequences would be that the people looked for a more pleasing form of poetic expression, in line with Shelley's understanding of its primal origins.

If Shelley emphasised the role of rhythm and pleasure in poetry Wordsworth stressed emotional authenticity and no-nonsense language in his 1801 'Preface to Lyrical Ballads'. 'All good poetry is the spontaneous overflow of powerful emotions'; 'I propose to… imitate … and to adapt' ... 'to bring my language close to the real language of men'. Like Shelley, he also thought that poetry was associated with a 'state of enjoyment' and 'complex feelings of delight'.

That emphasis on reflecting human reality reminds one of John Lennon's response to hearing Elvis Presley's 'Heartbreak Hotel', and rock music in general. 'Rock and roll was real, everything else was unreal. … You recognize something in it which is true …'

Which was a feeling that poetry in the style of 'The Waste Land', whatever its merits, did not produce. On the other hand, the new popular music that was developing and growing from the mid-20th century onwards, aided by technological breakthroughs and teenage spending power, did produce the pleasure, emotional authenticity and straightforward ways of expression that Shelley and Wordsworth had highlighted. How else can one explain the similar public reactions to the early deaths of Lord Byron in the 19th century and John Lennon in the 20th?

17

'And, in the end'

If the Younger Romantics are indeed 'the closest thing in history' to The Beatles it follows, because we can track their legacies and the influence they exerted, that we should be able to make some educated guesses about The Beatles and their future in the 21st century and beyond.

It's very possible, for example, that the group will find itself memorialised in Westminster Abbey, as Keats and Shelley were when a linked memorial plaque to Keats and Shelley was unveiled in 1955. Perhaps a similar tribute in Poet's Corner, or Liverpool Cathedral, will unite Lennon and McCartney at some point in the future.

Just as the Romantics have spawned a formidable international endeavour in the field of scholarship, so The Beatles are likely to make their presence felt in schools, universities and scholarly publications. My nephew, for example, 'did The Beatles' at his academy school in Hackney, the Department for Continuing Education at Oxford University is offering (as I write) a week long course on 'The Beatles, Popular Music and Sixties Britain', and the University of Liverpool (which has begun publishing a Journal of Beatles Studies) is advertising an MA degree in 'The Beatles: Music Industry and Heritage'. Beatles courses are also offered in the USA, and as the group offers such rich pickings for cultural historians, musicologists, specialists in poetry and literature and so on, the field of 'Beatles Studies' is bound to expand as time goes by and new perspectives emerge.

Just as the Romantics continue to feed the world of auctions so Beatles memorabilia will keep appearing too. In 2022 for example the Fine Books and Manuscripts Department at Bonhams in London offered a two-volume set of Italian poems (by the Tuscan poet Vincenzo da Filicaja) that Shelley gave to Claire Clairmont with an 'Extremely Rare Percy Bysshe Shelley Presentation Inscription' with an estimate of £60,000-80,000. And Lord Byron's continuing economic heft is demonstrated by the sale by a Los Angeles bookseller of a collection of 21 first editions of his work for £62,000, leading an online booksellers' listing of 'most expensive sales of April, May and June 2024' by quite a margin.

Craig Brown in '1234 Beatles' describes how even a piece of a ridiculous Beatles merchandise (a mocked up Beatles 'wig' in cardboard and iron filings) fetched over £1,000 at auction, and clearly more significant Beatles-related pieces will match or exceed those of the Romantics.

When there's money of this level involved Beatles forgeries are certain to appear, just as with the Romantics. In their case the most notorious examples being the Shelley publications and manuscripts produced in the late 19th century by the 'respected' Shelley scholars Thomas Wise and Harry Buxton Forman.

Forgers often try to fill a gap in the record; the 20th century Dutch collector, painter and forger Han Van Meegeren realised for example that there were no 'early Vermeers' so set out to make some himself. They were welcomed as a significant addition to the Vermeer catalogue, and he even succeeding in selling 'Christ and the Woman taken in adultery' to a certain Hermann Goering.

In the cases of Forman and Wise, they supplied the growing interest in Shelley by printing what appeared to be early editions of Shelley pamphlets and poems, and were protected from suspicion due to their genuine expertise. Their scams were only exposed in 1936, by two shrewd booksellers who had grown suspicious.

It follows that one area of focus for Beatles forgers could be the early years in Hamburg, when The Beatles were developing their craft. The only recordings from Hamburg are from their very last stint in the city at the Star Club, but the vital 'learning curve' gigs were unrecorded. Might someone, assisted by Artificial Intelligence and studio tech, succeed in mocking up some tracks to try to fill the gap?

The sheer creativity of the Romantic period also gives some perspective on the post-Sixties culture we inherit. Looking back, the 1960s cannot be regarded as anything but a creative high, with the slightly disconcerting implication that we live in an age of lesser individual talents. Where are the Dylans, the Hendrixes, the new Beatles? Leigh Hunt, who lived on for thirty five years after associating with the stellar talents of Keats, Shelley and Byron must have had a similar questions. Despite his friendship with (and respect for) poets and writers of the day such as Tennyson, the Brownings, Rossetti and Charles Dickens, they could not compare to the earlier poets who had been his companions.

When that next generation of British poets emerged they were living in an era that lacked the political intensity of the decades that opened the century. They also were part of a bigger and busier publishing culture, which had the effect of diluting the impact of their work. According to some estimates, in the years between 1802 and 1827, an average of 502 books were published annually. Britain's population stood at 11 million in 1801 but had risen to 21 million by 1851, and the number of annual publications was climbing towards 6,000 by 1900. It is easy to see that one book dropped into the relatively small pool of readers in the first decades of the 19th century would have a greater impact than a book published later in the century, when steam printing had greatly assisted the publishing industry, the railways had assisted the process of distribution, and the literate population had expanded hugely.

One is reminded of the record industry in 1967, when, as Elton John remembered, a new record, 'Sergeant Pepper', appeared in the window of his local music shop. It stayed there for six months, untroubled by any competition.

So the Victorian poets were working in a busier, more intellectually competitive environment, and as a result the overall social impact of their poetry could not be anything but diluted compared to their predecessors. They were big fish, true, but swimming in a large pool; Keats, Shelley and Byron were even bigger fishes, swimming in a smaller pool, and making bigger waves as a result. So the Victorians would look back to the Romantic era as a time of almost otherworldly achievement, as shown by Browning's famous lines from 'Suntreader':

> And did you once see Shelley plain –
> And did he stop and talk to you?

You could give that a modern twist, and it would sound just fine!

> And did you once see Hendrix plain?
> And did he stop and talk to you?

So – are we, here in the 21st century, in another era of 'dismal candles' – compared with the mega-talents and awesome cultural achievements of the 1960s? Some have no doubt, with the critic and author of 'Revolution in the Head' Ian MacDonald arguing in the mid-1990s that the music of the 1960s was 'on a higher level of achievement than today's' and that pop music arguably reached its highest point in late 1966, and had been in decline ever since.

Even if that is true, a more constructive assessment was voiced by Jefferson Airplane member Paul Kantner, offering another way to look at those luminaries of the past. Speaking to Jenny Boyd in the 1990s he argued that though 1960s culture had a coherence that was later dissipated, a development vastly increased in the internet age, its fragmentation had had a creative impact. It had been 'like a flower shooting pollen all over the place for new flowers to grow. Some of the new flowers are pretty ugly and some of them are quite beautiful. There's stuff to be had everywhere. There's just so much more of it, you're almost overloaded'. Which could also be a description of the post-Romantics culture as it lived on into the Victorian era, with the Romantics, like The Beatles, as the pollen helping to generate subsequent growth.

Though each of The Beatles, at one time or another, would say that they were 'just a rock 'n' roll band' such protestations never rang true. There was something else going on, as John Lennon sensed when he wondered if he would end up being compared to George Formby – or

Leonardo da Vinci. Could the Romantics also provide an understanding of The Beatles' true stature?

Parts of Shelley's essay 'A Defence of Poetry' do indeed spring to life if one understands The Beatles in light of the claims he makes for his broad, historically sweeping conception of poetry. For a start he defines poetry widely: in his eyes poetry is the expression of the imagination and is not confined to poetry alone. As the website of the Mustansiriyah University Baghdad puts it, Shelley 'considers that all are poets who express imagination in life; sculptors, artists, musicians, even lawgivers and the founders of religion, and all the arts are poetry' because of their imaginative function. The Beatles then, can be seen as part of that broad poetic tradition.

Then there is his famous formulation 'Poets are the unacknowledged legislators of the world'. Does that not now, over fifty years after their split, seem more and more appropriate to them? As Yoko Ono sang to her husband on 'Double Fantasy', his mind 'had changed the world'. A Shelleyan perspective might be that the Beatles songs we are so familiar with are like 'sparks' – or 'burning atoms' – 'of inextinguishable thought' that are scattered 'among mankind'. If Shakespeare plays are little worlds carrying meaning and multi-faceted perspectives into the future, so their songs continue that tradition in a new, contracted, form, adapted for new audiences and incorporating the rhythm and blues of the African-American soul.

Given The Beatles' focus on Love as a theme, most obviously when they sang 'All You Need Is Love' to a global audience in 1967, do they not unconsciously add themselves to Shelley's listing of poetic greats, who, since the eleventh century, beginning with the poetry 'of the Christian and chivalric eras', continuing through the Provençal troubadours and on to Petrarch and Dante, had championed Love? 'Love … has been celebrated by a chorus of the greatest writers of the renovated world … At successive intervals, Ariosto, Tasso, Shakespeare, Spencer, Calderon, Rousseau and the great writers of our own age, have celebrated the dominion of love, planting as it were trophies in the human mind of that sublimest victory over sensuality and force'.

Though one can find misogynistic elements in some Beatles songs, for example 'Run for Your Life' or 'You Can't Do That', the overall effect of their work, from 'She Loves You' through to 'Ticket To Ride' through to 'Don't Let Me Down' was to emphasise the importance of women's feelings, their agency and their centrality to happiness. Surely these songs have helped to establish greater gender equality in western and other cultures, and that that, too, would bear out Shelley's argument that poets are ultimately more influential than 'reasoners', important though their contribution is. They anticipated movements in consciousness in society and established them in people's minds. But they did this in a curious way, not by overt preaching but by bringing pleasure through their work, which, however, would go on to have a social and moral impact.

So that would go on to confirm another stage in his argument: 'Poetry strengthens the moral nature of man like exercise strengthens a limb'. 'It exceeds all imagination to conceive what would have been the moral condition of the world if neither Dante, Petrarch, Bocaccio, Chaucer, Shakespeare, Calderon, Lord Bacon, nor Milton had ever existed....' To that list The Beatles should assuredly be added.

It is tempting to argue that just as the socially visionary aspect of Shelley and Byron's work, (as well as the aesthetic sensibility of Keats) bore fruit in succeeding years so the peace campaigning aspect of Lennon's life and work will similarly have practical results. 'I have great hopes for my work' he said in one of final interviews; can those hopes be realised?

John Lennon asked us to imagine 'a brotherhood of man', with 'all the people living life in peace', drawing attention to an ideal world while living in one scarred by war and intolerance. 'Imagine' is mirrored by Shelley's bitter-sweet finale to 'Hellas', the poem he wrote following the outbreak of the Greek War of Independence. Beginning with

> The World's great age begins anew
>> The golden years return
> The earth doth like a snake renew
>> its winter weeds outworn

he ends up rebuking his own dreams:

> Oh cease! must hate and death return?
>> must men kill and die?
> Cease! drain not to its dregs the urn
>> Of bitter prophecy.
> The world is weary of the past,

Oh might it die or rest at last!

Shelley's scepticism is of course borne out by the continuation of war in the present day. The current war on Ukraine was started by someone seemingly immune to The Beatles' message of love: President Putin of Russia. Though attending a Paul McCartney concert in Moscow (and telling McCartney that The Beatles had been 'a first gulp of freedom') he revealingly declined to sing along with the supremely likeable end chorus to 'Hey Jude' and was most likely analysing the whole event with the calculating perspective learned in his KGB career. So W.H. Auden's dictum 'Poetry makes nothing happen' seems to be spot on.

Yet dreams of peace have been around for millennia: in the 8th century BCE Isaiah was writing 'they shall beat their swords into ploughshares, and their spears into pruning hooks; nation shall not lift up sword against nation, neither shall they learn war anymore'. In fact Shelley referred to Isaiah (and Virgil) when commenting on his lines from 'Hellas'. Noting that 'to anticipate however darkly a period of regeneration ... is a hazardous exercise' it nevertheless reminds 'the reader of Isaiah and Virgil, whose ardent spirits overleaping the actual reign of evil which we endure and bewail, already saw the possible and perhaps approaching state of society in which 'the lion shall lie down with the lamb ... Let these great names be my authority and my excuse'. So let them also be 'an authority and excuse' for John Lennon's 'Imagine', which updated and reimagined these visions within the new mass media environment of today's world. As another phrase from Shelley's notes on 'Hellas' puts it: 'It is the province of the poet to attach himself to those ideas which exalt and ennoble humanity'.

'Poets are the antennae of the race' John Keats wrote, and Shelley can be seen as a poet who picked up on the social changes of his era, such as the increasing energy available to humanity at the dawn of the industrial revolution and the increased demand for democratic rights in the emerging urban societies. Similarly Lennon picked up on the changes in twentieth century society, the world as a 'global village' as seen in NASA's photographs and the accompanying feeling that humanity could and should evolve away from warfare, and used them in his art.

One intriguing comparison between our era and that of the Romantics is found in the changes in moral codes that occurred as the Regency period turned into the Victorian era. Just as the freewheeling Regency period was succeeded by the rigid morality and accompanying hypocrisies of Victorian times, the similarly freewheeling attitudes of the 1960s have given way to the puritanical ethical codes of what its opponents call 'the new woke elite'. The rise of evangelism in Victorian times can, perhaps, be loosely equated with the rise of these contemporary moralists, dangling the same hopes of a re-ordered world but with the same blind spots, corruptions and accompanying hypocrisies as their Victorian predecessors. If history is a guide this new moralism will eventually be subjected to an Oscar Wilde-like scrutiny, which will act, as Byron wrote of the work of Cervantes, to 'smile Spain's chivalry away'.

Despite the problematic nature of Victorian morality, and its attendant social evils, the age was one of problem-solving, engineering feats and democratic advance in Britain. The era began with the widespread social disruption caused by the shift from an agriculturally-based economy to a new, increasingly industrialised society. The problems were formidable: widespread deprivation, overcrowded and unsanitary cities, unregulated housing, a 'democratic deficit', an absence of educational opportunities, desperate public health issues and so on. By the time of Queen Victoria's death in 1901 many of these issues had been addressed, to some extent at least. Mass literacy had been achieved, working class associations and civic groups that embedded social improvements had flourished, housing regulations had improved living standards, scientific advances had fed into engineering and medicine, and Britain was only 27 years away from achieving full democratic representation.

Will the post-Beatles era, with its own formidable set of difficulties, see those kinds of political and social advances on a global scale? It would be tempting to draw a direct line between our two eras but this would be to ignore the very real changes that have taken place. The sense of promise at the dawn of the industrial era has been succeeded by an encounter with the challenges it has spawned. The relatively coherent nation that was Victorian Britain (drawing on the benefits of industrialisation and Empire) has given way to a far more fragmented reality, fed by the destabilizing factors of climate change, population growth and migration. However, a hopeful perspective might be that the real benefits that came with the industrial revolution in post-Romantics Britain will find an echo in the global benefits from the digital revolution in the post-Beatles world.

In our post-Beatles world 'Poetry Proper' may be overshadowed by the drama, immediacy and financial power of the music industry but it would surely be wrong to think that it has lost its mojo forever. For there is a paradox: the poetry in rock 'n' roll is both weakened and strengthened by the addition of rhythm and melody. In a rock song, with all the instrumentation, harmonies, percussion and the impact of performance, the stricter standards of the written poem, 'wrestling with words and meaning', can be finessed; the poet with the blank page has no such back up: there is no hiding place.

Surely both media will continue as cousins, and both will have their time of triumph and popular impact. The standalone power central to poetry will keep recurring, as shown by Ronald Reagan's quotation (chosen by his speechwriter Peggy Noonan) from John Gillespie Magee's 'High Flight' in his speech made a mere five hours after the Challenger Space Shuttle disaster. A shocked national and international audience heard that the perished astronauts had 'slipped the surly bonds of earth to touch the face of God' and felt comforted, whatever their beliefs.

Another example stemmed from Richard Curtis's inclusion of W.H. Auden's poem 'Funeral Blues' in the funeral scene in 'Four Weddings and a Funeral'. 'Over to a better man' he said to himself as he was writing the scene, and the flamboyant Gareth was sent off to Auden's poem, spoken so memorably by John Hannah that each take held the audience of actors and extras spellbound. After proving equally mesmerising to film and television audiences, its publishers rushed out a best-selling Auden anthology to cater to popular demand, proving that 'Poetry Proper' can still fulfil the claims that Wordsworth, Keats and Shelley made for its continuing value.

Finally, can the Romantics give us any clues as to when 'the next Beatles' will arrive? One possibility might be that that the whole concept of the 'next Beatles' is now behind us, as they emerged from a time with a distinctive and unrepeatable combination of circumstances. Our era is one where the opportunities for online self-expression has created a proliferation and democratisation of individual talents.

Some speculate that, as one 'Eggpodder' said, they could have been a 'once in a century' phenomenon. Another contributor, John Higgs, floated the idea that just as we can see that there is Tudor Theatre, and Shakespeare as a one-off and towering part of it, perhaps future generations will see that there was Sixties Pop, and then there were The Beatles occupying the same position.

But the Romantics might yield one clue as to when 'the next Beatles' might arrive. As there were 151 years between the similar phenomena of Byron-mania (1812) and Beatle-mania (1963), if one draws a line between these two explosions of celebrity a similar amount of time may elapse before there is another similar sensation. Applying that calculation would give a date of 2121, and though it may be seen as ridiculous to make such a literalist prediction, it could be in the right sort of area.

To return to the comparison made at the outset between William Wordsworth and Elvis Presley: one can interpret that as a leap, across the centuries, of an artistic spirit based in feeling, rhythm and honest expression. They were the sparks that fired up firstly the Younger Romantics and secondly The Beatles, and who can say that a similar ignition will not occur at some point in the future?

If such a new phenomenon does emerge it will be unlikely to be working in the pure song format of The Beatles themselves. It would probably be some enhanced form of expression that would come as a surprise, 'stripping the veil of familiarity' from day to day life. After all, Beatles songs were augmented forms of poetic expression, using the power of music to give impetus to the stand-alone verses that had been Byron's medium. Another such progression would probably be needed to excite an audience well-used to the pop song format; it may also be that 'the next Beatles' emerges at a time of social stress where mass consciousness is in the kind of pent-up state that applied in the early 19th century and the 1960s.

What the situation will be in the 22nd century, if the 'Byron-Beatles calculus' holds, is anyone's guess, but the poet, in whatever form and all too likely shapeshifting anew, will reflect it and be part of it. To be, as Wordsworth wrote, a 'rock of defence for human nature; an upholder and preserver, carrying everywhere … relationship and love'.

APPENDIX 1
The Byron-Lennon book bonanzas

If evidence is needed for the connection made between the early deaths of Lord Byron and John Lennon one can find it in the extraordinary number of posthumous publications about them..

Medwin was well aware that there was a ready market for biographies and memoirs of the poet, and he scored an international hit with the book he worked up from his notes taken in Pisa. His 'Journal of the Conversations of Lord Byron' was published within months of Byron's death in April 1824 and became highly successful on an international basis, being published in Germany, France and Italy and going into twelve editions in the U.S.A.

Another book spawned in Pisa was Trelawny's own 'Recollections of the Last Days of Shelley and Byron' (1858) later revised and republished under the title 'Records of Shelley, Byron and the Author' in 1878. And the 18 months between Byron's departure from Pisa and his death in Missolonghi would yield the following published works about the poet, all incorporating reminiscences of Byron, perhaps based on only a day's acquaintance:

'A narrative of Lord Byron's Last Journey to Greece'
Count Pietro Gamba, (1825)
'Greece in 1823 and 1824' Colonel Leicester Stanhope,
(1824)
'The Last Days of Lord Byron', William Parry (1825)
'Lord Byron and some of his contemporaries', Leigh Hunt,
(1830)
'The Life of Lord Byron', John Galt, (1830)

228

'Conversations on religion with Lord Byron' Dr James
Kennedy, (1830)
'Memoirs of the affairs of Greece', Dr Julius Millingen,
(1831)
'Voyage from Leghorn to Cephalonia with Lord Byron',
James Hamilton Browne, (1834)
'The Idler in Italy' by Marguerite Lady Blessington,
(1839)
'A day with Lord Byron', George Bancroft, 1891

Like Thomas Medwin, Lennon's personal assistant
Fred Seaman had kept a diary about his days with the ex-
Beatle, and his memories, together with other recollections,
interviews, re-issues and biographies poured from the press:

'Borrowed Time' by Fred Seaman (1993)
'Dakota Days: The true story of John Lennon's final years'
by John Green (1983)
'Loving John' by May Pang, (1983)
'Strawberry Fields Forever: John Lennon
Remembered'(1980); Graustark, Garbarini, Cullman.
'The Lennon Tapes' (with Andy Peebles), (1981)
'The Playboy Interviews', (1982)
'The Lives of John Lennon', Ray Albert Goldman (1988)
'Lennon: The Definitive Biography', Ray Coleman (1995)
'Memories of John Lennon' edited by Yoko Ono (2005)
'John Lennon Summer of 1980' ed. Yoko Ono (1983) with
8 photographers
'One Day at a Time', Anthony Fawcett (reissued 1980)

There is also the case of the 'known unknown' –
each have a lost publication that could have added greatly to

our knowledge of their lives and careers. In Byron's case it was the destruction of his memoirs in his publisher's office. It would undoubtedly have been a good read; Thomas Medwin wrote that Byron told him that after 'a detailed account of my marriage and its consequences' its second section 'will prove a good lesson to young men; for it treats of the irregular life I led at one period, and the fatal consequences of dissipation. There are few parts that may not, and none that will not, be read by women. When you read my Memoirs you will learn the evils, moral and physical, of true dissipation. I can assure you my life is very entertaining and very instructive'. His friends however, believing it would damage his reputation, consigned it to the flames.

'What is the biggest unknown in the Beatles story?' the Beatles historian Mark Lewisohn was asked at an event in London in 2023. After thinking a while he replied that it must be the loss of Neil Aspinall's memories of the band. The ultimate Beatles insider, working with them as a roadie and driver from 1960 till 2007, his memories would have amounted, according to Lewisohn, to a 'golden key' that could have unlocked a multitude of questions and mysteries about the Beatles. After maintaining his silence for years Aspinall finally agreed, just before leaving for the United States, to talk extensively to him. One three hour interview, 'just scratching the surface', was recorded. But soon after he had left for the States Lewisohn got a message from one of his children: 'Dad's not well'. Shortly after he died of cancer: Neil Aspinall's memories were lost to history.

APPENDIX TWO:

'Shelley-Byron conversations in Pisa'

According to Thomas Medwin Shelley paid a regular one hour visit to Lord Byron in the Palazzo Lanfanchi in the early afternoon, and the subjects of their conversations can be guessed at:

- Pisa itself which for Byron 'had an Eastern air' and reminded him of his travels in Greece and Turkey;
- Italian poetry – Dante, Boccaccio etc. – possibly with mentions of Teresa whose love of the Italian classics had helped cement their relationship;
- The rising in Greece, Shelley's contacts with Greek exiles in Pisa, the liberality of the Tuscan government towards the exiles, Mary's study of Greek with the Greek patriot Prince Alexandrous Mavrocordato, Shelley's new work 'Hellas' inspired by the Greek insurrection, and the two poets' hopes for freedom in Italy;
- Byron's experiences of life in the Ottoman Empire with his description of his rescue of a young woman from execution in Athens and his inclusion in a British diplomatic meeting that had seen him entering the heart of the Ottoman power structure in Istanbul;
- Byron's impression of another despot during his travels in Albania, Ali Pasha, and (possibly) reactions to his death in January 1822;
- The merits or otherwise of Keats's work with his 'Hyperion' highly rated by the two but his other works less appreciated;

- Byron's involvement with the Gamba family and his experience of Italian family manners and sexual codes like that of the 'cavaliere servente';
- Southey's 'Satanic School' attack on the poets and their hoped for response through the journal;
- Hunt and his publisher brother John, with Byron realising that the increasingly daring tone of his work was leading to a break with his publisher John Murray and the new possibilities of being published through John Hunt;
- Reminiscences of their first encounter at the Villa Diodati in Switzerland with possible discussion of Mary's 'Frankenstein' and its publishing progress;
- The recent suicide of Dr Polidori who had been present there;
- Byron's plans to stage a Shakespeare play – Othello – at the Lanfranchi and who would fill the different roles;
- The merits of Shakespeare himself with Byron querying Shelley's reverential attitude to the bard;
- The Pisan Carnival with Shelley's puritanical reaction to the event contrasting with a more tolerant response from Byron;
- Life back in Britain with exchanges of news from various sources: 'How we used to laugh at what was grave in the suburbs!'

Select Bibliography

THE BEATLES:

Barrow, Tony, John, Paul, George, Ringo & Me. Andre Deutsch, 2005
Boyd, Jenny. It's not just rock 'n' roll. Jon Blake, 2013
Brown, Peter, and Gaines, Steven. The Love You Make. Pan, 1982
DeLillo, David. The Longest Cocktail Party. Canongate, 2005
Higgs, John Love and Let Die, Weidenfeld & Nicolson, 2022.
Kahn, Ashley (ed) George Harrison on George Harrison: Interviews and Encounters. Chicago Review Press, 2020
Lennon, John A Spaniard in the works
MacDonald, Ian. Revolution in the Head, Pimlico 1995
Sheff, David. The Playboy Interviews, New English Library, 1982

Online sources:

McCartney, Paul with Muldoon, Paul. The Lyrics podcast.
Shaw, Chris. I am the Eggpod.
The Beatles Bible.

THE ROMANTICS:

Baker, Carlos. Shelley's Major Poetry: The Fabric of a Vision. Princeton University Press, 1966.
Bone, Drummond (ed.) The Cambridge Companion to Byron, 2004.

Bredin, Hugh, and Santaro-Brienza, Liberato, Philosophies of Art and Beauty, Edinburgh University Press, 2000

Byron Letters. Everyman, 1971

Clark, David Leigh (ed), Shelley's Prose. The University of New Mexico Press, 1954.

Cronin, Richard Mapping Childe Harold I and II. The Byron Journal 1994.

Curry, Kenneth. Southey. Routledge, 1975

Gittings, Robert, and Manton, Jo. Claire Clairmont and the Shelleys. Oxford University Press, 1992.

John Keats Letters. Gowars and Grey, 1900.

Gilmour, Ian. Review of 'The Reading Nation in the Romantic Period' by William St Clair. London Review of Books, Vol 27, No 2, 2005.

Harding, Rosamund E.M. An Anatomy of Inspiration, Heffer and Sons, 1948

Holden, Anthony The Wit in the Dungeon: The Life of Leigh Hunt. Little, Brown, 2005.

Holmes, Richard. Shelley: the Pursuit. Harper Perennial, 2005.

Hunt, Thornton. 'Shelley, by One who Knew Him'. Atlantic Monthly 1863

F.L. Jones (ed) The Letters of Percy Bysshe Shelley Volumes I and II. Oxford University Press, 1964

F.L. Jones (ed) The Letters of Mary W. Shelley Volumes I and II. University of Oklahoma Press, 1946.

Langley Moore, Doris. Lord Byron Accounts Rendered. John Murray, 1974.

Leigh Hunt, James. The Autobiography of Leigh Hunt. Cresset Press, 1949

Lord Byron Don Juan. Penguin Books, 1973.

Lovell, David (ed). His Very Self and Voice Collected Conversations of Lord Byron. Macmillan, 1954.

Marchand, Leslie A. Byron A Portrait. John Murray, 1971.

Miller, Barnette, Leigh Hunt's relations with Byron, Shelley and Keats. The Columbia University Press, 1910.
Mole, Tom. What the Victorians Made of Romanticism. Princeton University Press, 2017.
Motion, Andrew. Keats. Faber & Faber, 2003.
Nicolson, Harold. The Last Journey. Constable, 1934
Norman, Sylva. The Flight of the Skylark. Max Reinhardt, 1954.
Parry, William. The Last Days of Lord Byron (1825)
Trelawny, Edward John. Records of Shelley, Byron and the Author. Penguin, 1973.
Shelley, Percy Bysshe. A Defence of Poetry and other Essays. Book Jungle, 2009.
Redpath, Theodore (ed.) Romantic Bards and British Reviewers. Harrap,1973
Reiman, Donald H., and Fraistat, Neil (eds) Shelley's Poetry and Prose. Norton, 2001
Shelley, Mary. Frankenstein. 1818.
Trelawny, Edward John. Recollections of Shelley, Byron and the Author
Walker, Carol Kyros. Walking North with Keats. Yale University Press, 1992.
Webb, Timothy. Religion of the Heart. Keats-Shelley Journal 1992.

Online sources:

Beaton, Roderick "What Byron really did for Greece and why it still matters" British school at Athens 2015,
https://www.bsa.ac.uk/videos/roderick-beaton-what-byron-really-did-for-greece-and-why-it-still-matters/
Peter Cochrane's website.
https://petercochran.wordpress.com/remembering-peter/tributes-to-peter-cochran/

Henderson, Graham. The Real Percy Bysshe Shelley.
http://www.grahamhenderson.ca/
Stabler, Jane. 'Religious Liberty in the 'Liberal.'
https://research-repository.st-
andrews.ac.uk/bitstream/handle/10023/5983/Stabler_2015
_BRANCH_Religious.pdf;jsessionid=17677374046B5DF05CE5
B27D0BE2F756?sequence=1
Romanticism and Wordsworth
http://mural.uv.es/guicarga/First%20Paper.htm

PART THREE:

Carey, John. The Intellectuals and the Masses. Faber & Faber,
1992
Carey, John. What Good Are the Arts? Faber & Faber, 2006
Hibberd, Dominic. Wilfred Owen: A New Biography. Ivan R.
Dee, 2003.
Pattison, Robert. The Triumph of Vulgarity: Rock Music in
the mirror of Romanticism. Oxford University Press, 1987.

References

Introduction

'The Beatles hadn't happened before' - Barrow, p. 250
'people 'were clamouring for freedom…' Miller, 1910.
'some great subterranean shift …' - Percy Bysshe Shelley,
Introduction to 'Prometheus Unbound'
'transcendent and culture-shifting…' - John Higgs, I am the
Eggpod No. 75.
'The poetry of earth is never dead' - John Keats, The Cricket
and the Grasshopper.

Chapter 1: From Tintern Abbey to Heartbreak Hotel

'John Lennon, listening to his radio in his bedroom at
night…' 'John Lennon Verbatim' BBC Radio
'Elvis was the thing ….'I wanted to be Elvis'-
https://daytrippin.com/2018/10/08/john-lennons-lifelong-
obsession-with-elvis-presley/
George Harrison on Elvis - Kahn, Ashley, 2020
Paul McCartney on Elvis - Speaking backstage in Memphis
Tennessee 2005
'the emphasis on 'order, logic, balance, propriety, reason and
mastery of the emotions'. Romanticism and Wordsworth
http://mural.uv.es/guicarga/First%20Paper.htm
'acquired, for two guineas - Wordworth's The Excursion…' -
Gilmour, 2005.
Colin Silver, Wordsworth and Keats -
http://wordsworth.org.uk/blog/2014/10/25/wordsworth-and-
keats/

Leigh Hunt on Wordsworth - *The Examiner* 1.6.1817
https://lordbyron.org/doc.php?choose=LeHunt.1817.Keats1.x
ml
See also Holden p.94
'one feeling from the beginning of the visit – Lovell, p. 129
Beatles meeting with Elvis – Barrow, p.143.
"I met him in Madison Square Garden …'Far out magazine
https://faroutmagazine.co.uk/george-harrison-disappointed-
with-elvis/
'perhaps the most expensive work of literature ever published
in England' - Gilmour, 2005.
Byron Wordsworth Review, Life of Lord Byron, Thomas
Moore, Vol. VI, Misc. Prose. - Review Of Wordsworth's
Poems,
'Used to dose me with Wordsworth physic…' Medwin, 1824.
'What a beastly and pitiful wretch that Wordsworth!' - Letters
II, 25.7.1818
'a Wordsworth he admired and a Wordsworth for whom he
felt a profound distaste' - Clarence D Thorpe
https://www.jstor.org/stable/457549)
'I met him in Madison Square Garden…' – Far Out Magazine
21.6.2022.
 'Byron, Shelley and Leigh Hunt are to lay their heads
together in some town in Italy…' Quoted in Stabler, Jane
https://branchcollective.org/?ps_articles=jane-stabler-
religious-liberty-in-the-liberal
'The Beatles came to America…
https://faroutmagazine.co.uk/elvis-presley-the-beatles-
ruining-america/
That's very sad to me, that he felt so threatened..' IMDb
Ringo Starr quotes
https://www.imdb.com/name/nm0823592/quotes/
'he ended up a complete plonker...' Paul McCartney 1994
quoted in The Daily Express

https://www.express.co.uk/entertainment/music/1900806/Elvi
s-army-Paul-McCartney-John-Lennon-Beatles
   'Our different parties' – A Vision of Judgment, Stanza 42.
George Harrison 'We still love him and he's still there in his
spirit ….' Creem magazine, 1988.

Chapter 2: Inspiration from Plato to Pop

'To Dave Sholin and Laurie Kaye he said …'
http://www.beatlesarchive.net/john-lennons-last-interview-
december-8-1980.html
'Across the Universe' - John Lennon, Playboy interview
http://www.beatlesinterviews.org/db1980.jlpb.beatles.html
'The mind in creation…' – Percy Bysshe Shelley, A Defence
of Poetry
'Ion' begins with Socrates meeting …' 'Ion; or, of the Iliad' -
translation by Percy Bysshe Shelley
'Byron's writing begins and thrives in disillusion' –
McGann, quoted in Cambridge Companion to Byron pp.222-
3
'If Byron were inspired with Socrates' divine madness…'.
Trelawny. p.99
'The mischief that lurks in all Lord Byron's productions is
this….' Redpath, p. 258.
'Byron's wit and humour …' Trelawny, p. 103.
'hope is a solemn duty…' Letters II p.125.
'I am like a tyger in poesy…' To John Murray, September 18,
1820. He is also quoted as saying: "All convulsions end with
me in rhyme'.
Richard Woodhouse on Keats cited by Melissa Love Koenig
at https://law.marquette.edu/facultyblog/2013/04/keats-and-
the-lawyer/
Paul McCartney on writing 'Yesterday'
http://www.beatlesebooks.com/yesterday

'Another theory, attributed to the French novelist Alphonse Daudet…' Harding, p.106
'F*** a pig it's Paul!' Quoted by personal assistant Fred Seaman

Chapter 3: Byronic fame and Beatlemania

'I thought it was pretty strange why we made the enormous impact…' Copyright © Jenny Boyd, 2023. 'It's Not Only Rock 'n' Roll' First published in the UK by John Blake, an imprint of Bonnier Books UK Ltd
Paul McCartney "It was thrilling, terrifying.…' ABC interview.
November 26, 2009
'Childe Harold' 'Its first deluxe edition 'sold its complete run…' - McClay, Gramma: History of Theory and Criticism
https://ejournals.lib.auth.gr/gramma/article/view/6280/6030
'Mapping *Childe Harold* I and II', Richard Cronin, *The Byron Journal, Volume 22*, Copyright © 1994 The Byron Society, Published by Liverpool University Press
https://doi.org/10.3828/BJ.1994.1
'The subject of conversation, of curiosity…' Cronin, 1994.
I am the Eggpod No 111. Meet the Beatles with Christine Feldmann-Barrett.
Mick Jagger quoted in - https://faroutmagazine.co.uk/the-rolling-stones-classic-mick-jagger-chuck-berry/
Noel Coward, Christian Science Monitor 2012
https://www.csmonitor.com/Books/2012/0806/Hello-Goodbye-Hello-6-oddball-meetings-between-celebrities/Paul-McCartney-and-Noel-Coward
Wordsworth on Childe Harold, 17. 5.1818 to Mary Wordsworth
Walter Scott on Childe Harold, Cronin, 1994.

'Lord Byron is in this respect fortunate....' Letters II. p. 436, 18.6.1822. But Byron would make a shrewd comment on fame and its attendant responsibilities and hazards when he said to Lady Blessington in Genoa: 'Shelley had been tried in the school of adversity only, which is not such a corrupter as is that of prosperity'.

Chapter 4: Come Together ... over Leigh

Paul McCartney on Ringo, New Musical Express 19.4.2015
https://www.nme.com/news/music/ringo-starr-7-1214353
https://www.cheatsheet.com/entertainment/moment-paul-mccartney-knew-ringo-starr-perfect-drummer-beatles.html/
'Ringo was a star in his own right ...' John Lennon, The Playboy Interviews.
The American edition of 'The Story of Rimini', Leigh Hunt, Autobiography p.259.
'scandalous and defamatory libel', Holden. p 72.
'what Shelley called 'that great poem' – A Defence of Poetry.

Chapter 5: Two of Us: Hunt and Byron in England

'If the political scene seemed grim', Holden, p. 92.
Byron's 'tactful expressions in the margins', Marchand, p.202.
'When a man talks of system...', Marchand, p.283.
Byron recommends the Story of Rimini to Murray - Byron to Murray, Letters, Nov. 1815.
'Hunt was the only man...', Holden, p. 103.
'Many ladies accoutred themselves as chambermaids...', Marchand p. 234.
'To hail the laurelled bard...', Gittings, pp.109-10.

'Lord Byron is an exceedingly interesting person…', Holmes, p. 337. See Buxton, p. 26 for an interpretation of Shelley's comment.

'Shelley had 'discovered in his second wife…', Sperry, Shelley's Major Verse, p. 41.

John Lennon 'the rest is history…', The Playboy Interviews.

Manfred quote Omar Miranda Romantic Circles website https://romantic-circles.org/praxis/manfred/praxis.2019.manfred.intro.html

'Why do you call yourself an atheist ?', Trelawny, p. 107.

'And they came to him for all quarters…', Mark 1:4

'The plurality of worlds …', Queen Mab, Notes. NOTE: Another note from Queen Mab, 'There is no God', is immediately qualified by a thought taken from Sir William Jones's studies of Indian thought and culture, providing a link to the The Beatles' own contact with Indian culture and philosophy. 'This negation must be understood solely to affect a creative Deity. The hypothesis of a pervading Spirit co-eternal with the universe remains unshaken'.

'the interfused and overruling Spirit …', 'Essay on Christianity', David Lee Clark p. 201.

a 'light of enchantment that can never be dissolved', Buxton, p.55.

'Chapman, a contemporary of Shakespeare, had translated a section of Homer's Odyssey…' - see John Keats vs. The Enlightenment by Paul Gallagher, Schiller Institute https://archive.schillerinstitute.com/fid_91-96/963_keats.html

'We became friends on the spot…', Holden, p. 105.

'Keats was suddenly made a familiar of the household…', Gittings, p. 132.

'This sealed his fate…' - Discussed at https://www.poetryfoundation.org/poets/john-keats

Keats and Shelley meeting - Leigh Hunt, Autobiography, pp.273-4 and Gittings, p. 174.
'Leigh Hunt has been with me all day,…' Shelley to Mary, Letters I, 16.12.16.
Note : 'Medwin said that Shelley told him that …', Buxton, p. 57.
Hunt and Shelley, Holden, p. 108 .
'I never took up the lancet again', Gittings, p. 132.
Abbey's account of meeting with Keats, Gittings, p.152-3.
Thomas Moore Wordsworth quotation on Childe Harold - https://www.jstor.org/stable/30212718

Chapter 7: A Year in the Life

'With graceful flowers tastefully placed about…', Shelley, Letter to Maria Gisborne.
'Sappho's meek head…', Sleep and Poetry, lines 353-404.
Keats's poem was called 'On Receiving a Laurel Crown from Leigh Hunt' while Hunt produced 'On Receiving a Crown of Ivy from John Keats'.
'this complete and highly-finished work…', Gittings, p.166.
'even published his own in *The Examiner*…', Holden, p.119.
Note : 'Medwin said that Shelley told him that The Revolt of Islam arose from an agreement with Keats that each should write a long poem within six months', Buxton p. 57.
'a brother and sister who 'inspire and lead a bloodless revolution…', p. 101, Shelley's Poetry and Prose, Norton.
'we are somewhat embarrassed about her. We are exposed to…', Letters, 1, p. 547.
 '…to have an unaccountable infant in their home …', Gittings and Manton, pp.37-38
she 'talked herself into handing her over to him', Lesley McDowell, Wordsworth Trust blog,

https://wordsworth.org.uk/blog/2014/03/28/claire-clairmont-on-her-letters-and-journals/
'I have read Manfred with the greatest admiration. ...',
Letters 1, 9.7.1817.
'my long poem under the title 'The Revolt of Islam' ...',
Letters I, 17.12.1817.
'...for which he would demand the princely sum of £2,625',
Curry, Kenneth p. 17 .
'With one stroke he freed himself from the fetters of British
propriety ...', Marchand, p. 273.
'splendid insights', Brian Fallon, Foreword to 'Philosophies
of Art and Beauty', p. xi
'his sale of Newstead Abbey...' Discussed by Christine
Kenyon Jones in 'Byron and Slavery' at
https://www.liverpooluniversitypress.co.uk/doi/10.3828/bj.20
23.16

Chapter 8: 'I'll follow the Sun'

John and Yoko's concerns about Kyoko
https://news.amomama.com/252609-yoko-onos-lost-
daughter.html
"But who's afraid? ...', John Keats, Letters 23.1.1818
'found it somewhat bewildering'..., , Buxton, p. 59.
Hunt's version is 'competent ... Keats's and Shelley's betray
embarrassment', Holmes, p. 410
'Byron used to lament that he could not versify as well as
Shelley', Lovell, p. 217.
'while Hunt's version is 'competent ...', Holmes, p. 410.
'which was popularly supposed to have caused Keats's death
that he could fathom it', *Atlantic Monthly*, XI, p. 406. Quoted
in Barnette Miller,
https://www.gutenberg.org/files/35733/35733-h/35733-
h.htm#f509_509

'as Peter Cochran noted' -
https://petercochran.wordpress.com/
…banned in Italy under Austrian rule …'
https://petercochran.files.wordpress.com/2009/03/chp4.pdf).
'His condition was never quite the same…', Walker, p.5
'at a loss to understand Scott's embarrassment…' Joseph
Severn, writing in The Atlantic Monthly, April, 1863
'Where are we going, fellows?...' Far Out magazine 7.3.2023

Chapter 9: The 'Sergeant Pepper Year'

Note: A line from Shelley's prose mirrors almost exactly the
first line of ''I Am The Walrus'': 'I am he as you are he as
you are me And we are all together'. Shelley wrote, in his
essay 'On Life': 'The words *I*, and *you*, and *they* are
grammatical devices invented simply for arrangement, and
totally devoid of the intense and exclusive sense usually
attached to them'.
'a piece of Regency slang …', Lord Byron Don Juan, p. 564.
'…if people won't discover the moral, that is their fault',
Marchand, p. 293.
'You won't make Canticles of my cantos …', Marchand, p.
294.
Don Juan 'too free for these modest days', Marchand,
pp..287-93.
'You who are my only and last love…', Lord Byron Don
Juan p.602
'He commented gloomily' …'You see what it is to be under
six feet and not a Lord', Gittings, p. 426.
'It would be just as well to trounce Lord Byron', Letters,
April 1819.
'one of the most important poetic works ever published...',
Kelvin Everest, quoted in Wikipedia
https://en.wikipedia.org/wiki/John_Keats

'Methinks it is a wonderful work for a girl of nineteen…',
Letters, 15th May 1819.
'the blogger Erich Kuersten…' -
https://acidemic.blogspot.com/2012/11/a-hole-in-me-pocket-
beatles-est-buddha.html
'..topped with an upper room' - https://www.alamy.it/foto-
immagine-villa-valsovano-scrittura-luogo-di-percy-shelley-s-
cenci-nei-pressi-di-monte-nero-livorno-ex-livorno-in-inglese-
italia-83356863.html
'I wait anxiously to hear how the Country will express …',
Letters II, p. 117.
'Write to me quickly what you think of this plan ….' Letters
II p.67.
'I had been thinking about it up in the hills in India…', The
Beatles 2000, p.298.
Shelley and nonviolence - George Ewane Dgidi,
'Romanticism and Nonviolence: Percy Bysshe Shelley
Exhumed' International Journal of Literature and Arts 2024;
Vol. 12, No. 2, pp. 16-26
https://doi.org/10.11648/j.ijla.20241202.11f
'…in a 'state for the best sort of poetry', Gittings, p 497.
'I thought it was about time … I had been thinking about it up
in the hills in India'
https://en.wikipedia.org/wiki/Revolution_(Beatles_song)#cite
_note-FOOTNOTEThe_Beatles2000298-18
'I was so fed up I didn't bother to contact the others…'
https://www.beatlesbible.com/1960/12/10/john-lennon-
leaves-hamburg/

Chapter 10: 'There's a shadow hanging over me'

My grandfather gave me a harmonica ... " The Beatles. 2000,
p.36 .

'On human capital' -
https://www.worldbank.org/en/publication/human-
capital/brief/about-hcp
'Ringo's presence ensured that, however far they
ventured…', Gould, pp.127-8.
'he had been removed from his lodgings in the
neighbourhood…', Letters, II, p. 220.
Keats prose pieces from Essay in *The Indicator*
'if it does not sell well, I think nothing will ever sell again',
Gittings, pp. 581-2.
 'has had a moderate sale', Gittings, p.583.
'he will attain an exalted and a lasting station among English
poets', Redpath, pp. 372
- '…asking for 'patience at my lunes…', Motion, p.527.
'Here are Johnny Keats's piss a-bed poetry ….', Byron to
John Murray, 4th October 1820.
'…is based on a paltry originality…', Marchand, p. 91.
'You, John, have so many friends…', Gittings, p. 550.
'he is destined to become one of the first writers of the
age'…, Letters II, 9.10.1820.
Shelley to Peacock Letters II, pp. 244 and 262.
He had told Marianne Hunt 'His other things are imperfect
enough…', Letters II p. 238
Where did you learn all these secrets? I should like to go to
school there' Letters II, p. 198.
That her disappointment should vex her…' Letters II, pp.
235-6.

Chapter 11: 'Now in the realm of light'

'We are not rich enough for that sort of thing…', Letters II,
18/2/1821 p. 268.
'Poor Keats! They sent word from Rome that he is dying…',
Letters II, p. 280

'tell that poet and noble-hearted man', Leigh Hunt to Joseph Severn, 8.3.1821
I am afraid poor fellow that it is too late', Letters II, p. 281
'…the putting of Allegra, at her years, in a convent …' Gittings and Manton, p. 59
'she intreats you to believe that she is most anxious to show it', Letters II, p. 283
'I am very sorry to hear what you say of Keats...', Byron to Shelley 26.4.1821
'It is transparent … that Shelley was not thinking in any realistic way…', Holmes, p. 648.
'I know what to think of Adonais', Letters II, April 10th 1822.
'…I send it to the press here, & you will soon have a copy', Letters II, p. P. 302
'…I have cancelled in the preface the whole passage…', Letters, II, p. 306.
'& that it was more an elegy on himself than the subject of it', Webb, p. 49.
'Described by Paul as a 'memories song …', McCartney, A Life in Lyrics. https://www.pushkin.fm/podcasts/mccartney-a-life-in-lyrics/here-today
'The 2nd century 'Lament for Bion'…', text translated/re-imagined by Henry Alford (1810-71).
Also to be mentioned is Ringo's song 'Imagine Me There'.
'…I have received a most melancholy account…', Letters II, p.302
'…that it was more an elegy on himself …', Webb, p. 49.

Chapter 12: An Italian Apple

'Apple was a noble experiment that failed', DiLello, p.xi
'According to Cynthia Lennon, when The Beatles stopped touring …', A Twist of Lennon, p. 146

Lennon and McCartney on the formation of Apple at
https://en.wikipedia.org/wiki/Apple_Corps#cite_note-
LennonMcCartneyTonightShow-8
And https://en.wikipedia.org/wiki/Apple_Corps#cite_note-
LennonMcCartneyApplePressConference-21
'…every window of the inn was open to see him', Marchand,
p. 355.
'new book on Byron…', John Watkins, 'A Historical and
Critical Memoir of the Life and Writings of Lord Byron',
1822.
'The Palazzo Lanfranchi on the Lung' Arno in Pisa, a
building not unlike the Apple HQ at 3 Savile Row' - see
https://www.thefirstfabfour.co.uk/index.php/gallery
 '….a small body has already been raised…', Edward
Williams, quoted by Lovell p. 265.
'Shelley's earnestness and just criticism …', Trelawny p.71
'Shelley was what Byron could not be…', Lovell, p. 273.
Medwin on Byron and Shelley, Lovell, p. 273.
Byron thought his philosophy too spiritual …', Lovell, p. 310.
'…it is well for us to know what we should avoid no less than
what we should seek', Letters, II, p.358.
has produced a chaos of perplexities…', Letters, II, p. 379.
'an appendix to his play 'The Two Foscari' …' -
https://petercochran.wordpress.com/wp-
content/uploads/2009/03/the_two_foscari.pdf
"You have not seen my Vision of Judgement.", Medwin,
quoted in Lovell, p.120.
'…He is forever dilating upon his impatience …' Letters II,
2.3.1822
"The truth is, my dear Moore,…', Byron Letters 4.3.1822
'many difficulties have presented themselves…', Letters II
25.1.1822.
'this last discussion about money particularly so', Letters II
17.2.1822

'taking 'a tight-lipped leave of Lord Byron …..', Holmes, p 712.

'she has sustained her loss with more fortitude ..'Letters I, 1.5.22

'Lord Byron felt the loss at first bitterly…' Mary Shelley Letters I, 139 p. 169

'To Leigh Hunt Esq., in admiration of ….', Holden, p. 155.

'an impossible prolongation of fleeting intervals of beauty and joy', Crook, Nora, p. 3

'would not hear of the charitable remarks of Lord Byron…', Lovell, p. 301.

'scudding into the harbour of Livorno…', Trelawny, p 153.

'Lord Byron is at this moment on the point of leaving Tuscany', Letters II p. 444

He was 'inexpressibly glad…', Thornton Hunt, 1863.

'he seems inclined to depart without the necessary explanations…', Letters II, p. 444

'noting the atmosphere of 'active movement …', vigour and decision that surrounded him', Thornton Hunt, 1863.

'His friend had marked, all through the volume, the passages that…', Webb, p.47.

When I told him his lip quivered …', Trelawny pp. 159-60.

'folded open at 'Lamia…', Holden, p. 164.

'I firmly believe it was the CIA along with the FBI who murdered John Lennon….'
https://www.wattpad.com/560443848-music-conspiracy-theories-was-john-lennon-murdered

'their feelings are easily excited into sympathy….', Trelawny p.171.

'open, and doubled back…', Webb, p. 36.

Chapter 13: 'You never give me your money'

'Mafia here!' the Apple Scruffs would shout….', Brown,
Gaines p. 311.
'He knows everything about us…', Get Back, Episode 3.
 'Byron assured Hunt that 'he would stand in Mr Shelley's
place', Holden, p. 169.
'We then lounged about, or stayed and talked…', Lovell, p.
319.
'the sort of poetry in which he excelled…', Lovell, p. 310.
'the feeling of joy that had once pervaded the building …',
Brown, Gaines p. 311.
'What does Hunt want with the heart?' asked Byron, Medwin,
Lord Byron and his Times.
'I must trouble you for another 'cool hundred' of your
crowns', Marchand, p.390
'It is the first time I ever heard of them…', Holden p. 173.
'a recent sketch of Byron made him 'look like a great
schoolboy…', Holden p. 174.
Teresa wrote that 'If Byron appeared ….', Holden p. 174.
'assisting Hunt, he wrote, was 'like pulling a drowning man
out of a river…', To Thomas Moore, 2.5.1823.

Chapter 14: Give Greece back to the Grecians

'Besides, who would ever shave themselves in such a state?',
To Thomas Moore, 5.7.1821.
'noted for his 'cruelty, bravery, guile and cupidity…',
Langley Moore, p.188
'the Greeks appear in more danger…', To Hobhouse,
11.9.1823.
'I think it a thousand pities that …', Langley Moore, p. 390.
Note: The Casa Aulla Pisa, where Mary swapped language
lessons with a Greek prince, Shelley first heard of the death

of Keats, and wrote his essay 'A Defence of Poetry', is now the Royal Victoria Hotel.

'relief from this hell...', Langley Moore, p. 382.

'that was nearly all the comfort his deplorable room...', Parry, The Last Days of Lord Byron.

'Beware your 37th year, my young Lord!', Millingen, pp. 128-34, 140-4.

'a funeral oration was delivered' (by M. Spiridon Tricoupi). Tennyson wrote 'Byron is dead'....', Marchand, p. 467.

'John Clare, in London's Tottenham Court Road...', Clare, John, 'Byron's Funeral'

'Now has descended a serener hour', The Revolt of Islam, stanza 9.

'then unfashionable watchwords' See Jon Landau's review of 'Ram' at https://www.rollingstone.com/music/music-album-reviews/ram-105109/ which, with its puritanical air, could be compared to the spirit animating Lockhart's 'Endymion' review.

Chapter 15: 'The Long and Winding Road'

Keats death messaging traced by Nicholas Roe
https://www.thebritishacademy.ac.uk/podcasts/10-minute-talks-death-john-keats-early-reputation/

The Real John Bull, who, as Sylva Norman noted', Norman, p. 16.

'without Mary's editorial intervention ...', Alegre, Sara Martín, Percy Bysshe Shelley: Thanks to Mary's Love.
https://webs.uab.cat/saramartinalegre/2019/03/25/percy-bysshe-shelley-thanks-to-marys-love/

'Within a few weeks of PBS's death...', Mercer, Rethinking the Collaborative Literary Relationship of Percy Bysshe Shelley and Mary Wollstonecraft Shelley

https://etheses.whiterose.ac.uk/18022/1/PhD%20postVIVA%20Anna%20Mercer.%20Submitted%20Aug%202017.pdf
'the Shelleys' …history of …shared activities…' Robinson, Charles
http://shelleygodwinarchive.org/contents/frankenstein/the-frankenstein-notebooks-introduction/#mws_and_pbss_collaboration_in_the_frankenstein_notebooks
'Sir T. writhes under the fame of his incomparable son…', Mary Shelley, Letters I, p. 302.
'a droll circumstance', Shelley to John Gisborne, June 16th, 1821.
'the revolutionary Queen Mab was sold cheaply…', Gilmour, 2005.
'Shelley's name was assured currency …', Holmes, p. 662.
'…the Harvard Gazette…' August 2001.
'They sit over a shivering fire …', Holden, p. 201.
'Sonnet to Percy Shelley', Holden, p. 190.
'the poet's work was effectively out of print' Plumly, Stanley p. 70.
Rossetti https://victorianweb.org/authors/dgr/bottai1.html
'The Unborn Byron', Ça Va by Slapp Happy, writer Peter Blegvad.
'Alice in Wonderland' was one of the books …', Rolling Stone 6.5.75
'now an 'old man with snowy hair…', Holden, p. 333
'dismal candles' – 'the great Victorians Hunt knew well, but they flicker like dismal candles … after Shelley's bright flame'. Morpurgo, p.xxiv
'the Romantics were renovated …' Mole, Tom, 2017.
'Walt Whitman was one of its readers…' Dowden's biography also provoked Mark Twain's essay 'In Defence of Harriet Shelley'. Another American author contributing to

Romantics' criticism at the time was Harriet Beecher Stowe
who published 'Lady Byron vindicated' in 1870.
'The publication of Keats's letters to Fanny Brawne...',
Łuczyńska-Hołdys, Małgorzata, 2012.
'Byron became the symbolic icon of British Romanticism'
from 'The Byronic Myth in Brazil: Cultural Perspectives on
Lord Byron's Image in Brazilian Romanticism', Matthew
Lorin Squires, Brigham Young University, 2005.
'Matt Sandler's demonstration that an 'extraordinary array' of
African-American writers...' in the Byron Journal, 45.1
(2017). From 'Byron and Slavery' op cit.
Shelley 'was a favourite of the Pankhurst family ...', Foot, p.
156.
'New York trade unionist Pauline Newman was inspired by
Shelley ...', Graham Henderson, The Real Percy Bysshe
Shelley website.
'This volume leaves out *all* Shelley's contentious poems...',
Foot p. 248.

Chapter16: *'The Long and Winding Road' II*

'Matthew Arnold, who had labelled him...', Arnold,
Matthew, Essays in Criticism: Second Series,1888.
Scarriet website -
https://scarriet.wordpress.com/2012/03/04/free-love-percy-
shelley-and-t-s-eliot/CHAPTERSEVENTEEN
Morris Dickstein on F.R. Leavis, New York Times, June 22,
1975.
'Shelley was snuffed out in the 1950s and 1960s ...', Foot,
pp. 261-262. But Nora Crook notes that as a contrarian Leavis
provoked some useful reactions, including from those who
correlated meteorological phenomena with the 'Ode to the
West Wind'.
'The mass of capabilities remains at every period materially
the same...', from the preface to 'Prometheus Unbound'.

'Our normal word for things that cannot be understood ….'
Carey, John, What Good are the Arts?, p. 47.
''Romanticism lived on in the schoolroom as in the life of the
South… 'Pattison, p.52.
'Rock 'n' roll was real….' Rolling Stone issues # 74 & 75
21 Jan & 4 Feb, 1971
Chapter 17: 'And, in the end'

'two shrewd booksellers who had grown suspicious…',
https://www.theatlantic.com/magazine/archive/1945/02/thom
as-j-wise-and-his-forgeries/656565/
'…the number of publications was on the way towards
reaching 6,000 by 1900',
https://www.britannica.com/topic/publishing/Spread-of-
education-and-literacy
'the music of the 1960s was 'on a higher level of achievement
than today's' MacDonald, p. 299
'Paul Kantner speaking to Jenny Boyd…', Boyd, Jenny,
2013. Copyright © Jenny Boyd, 2023. 'It's Not Only Rock
'n' Roll' First published in the UK by John Blake, an imprint
of Bonnier Books UK Ltd.
Bonhams auction
https://www.bonhams.com/press_release/34056/
'an online booksellers' listing of 'most expensive sales…'
https://www.abebooks.co.uk/books/rarebooks/most-
expensive-sales-april-may-june-2024
'… considers that all are poets who express imagination in
life …' Mustansiriyah University Baghdad
https://uomustansiriyah.edu.iq/media/lectures/8/8_2022_05_2
8!11_17_28_PM.pdf
'as Byron wrote of the work of Cervantes…', Don Juan Canto
13 Stanza 11.
'just as we can see that there is Tudor Theatre …', John
Higgs, I am the Eggpod No. 75.

'Bringing everywhere relationship and love ….',
Wordsworth, William, Preface to Lyrical Ballads, 1802.

Appendix 1: The Byron-Lennon book bonanzas

'I can assure you my life is very entertaining and very instructive…', Byron's Memoirs, Wikipedia https://en.wikipedia.org/wiki/Byron%27s_Memoirs#cite_note -FOOTNOTEKnight2016214-36

'Beatles historian Mark Lewisohn was asked …' - https://iamtheeggpod.com/2023/07/09/eggpod-live-at-opera-holland-park-part-2/

INDEX

Sergeant Pepper's Lonely Hearts
Club Band, 215; 'She Loves
 You', 218; 'Something', 103;
'Strawberry Fields Forever', 100,
115; 'The Long and Winding
Road', 113; 'Tomorrow Never
Knows', 63; 'This Boy', 30;
'Ticket To ride', 218; 'Yellow
Submarine', 194; 'Yesterday', 21,
113; 'You Can't Do That', 218;
streams on Spotify, 197

Blackwood's Magazine, 68, 87,
89
Blegvad, Peter, 252
Boileau, Pierre, 65
Bowie, David, 114
Boyd, Jenny, 24, 216
Boyd, Patti, 24
Brawne, Fanny, 117, 121, 123,
125, 130, 185, 196
Brougham, Henry, 10, 86
Brown, Charles Armitage, 85, 86,
98, 118, 120, 130, 185, 190
Brown, Craig, 213
Brown, Peter, 170
Browning, Elizabeth Barratt, 179
Browning, Robert, 215
Burns, Robert, 85
Buxton Forman, Harry, 213

Byron, George Gordon, Lord

and the Greek War of
Independence, 174; attacks
Keats, 124; Byron-
mania, 26, 41, 60, 150; 'could not
versify as well as Shelley', 77,
152; helps Leigh Hunt with 'The
Story of Rimini', 40; in
Missolonghi, 177;involvement
with Carbonari, 118; leaves
Britain, 44; meeting with
Wordsworth, 8; moves to
Ravenna, 118; offers to fund
Leigh Hunt's journey to Italy, 97;
on 'Hyperion', 141; on
'Frankenstein', 104; on
inspiration, 20; on Leigh Hunt,
84; on Wordsworth, 7; pledges
support to Hunt in Pisa, 169;
publication of 'Beppo', 77;
puzzled by Keats's 'beaker full of
the warm South', 169; queries
Shelley's account of Keats's
 death, 135; responds to
Southey's 'Satanic School' attack,
156; response to 'The Revolt of
Islam', 76; response to death in
Britain, 178; visits Leigh Hunt in
prison, 37

Works

'Beppo', 77, 144; 'Childe Harold's
Pilgrimage', 19, 25-8, 32, 49, 56,
59, 71, 77, 81, 114, 150, 198;
'Childe Harold's Pilgrimage',
Italian translation, 83;
'Darkness', 50, 61; 'Detached
Thoughts', 147; 'Don Juan', 19,
53, 84, 96 101, 111, 126, 142,
154 169, 190; 'English Bards and
Scotch Reviewers', 7; 'Fare Thee

Well', 41; 'Manfred', 50, 67, 150; 'Mazeppa', 19; 'The Prisoner of Chillon', 50; 'The Prophecy of Dante', 22, 102, 146, 150; 'The Curse of Minerva', 193; 'The Two Foscari', 156; 'The Vision of Judgement', 14, 19, 151, 157, 164, 171; verses on Keats, 141, 142

Calderon, 218
Cameron, Kenneth, 206
Campbell, Glenn, 88
Carey, John, 206, 208
Carlile, Richard, 189
Carlyle, Thomas, 179
    on *The Examiner*, 85
Carroll, Lewis, 194
Cervantes, 221, 254
Chapman, George, 54
Charles, Ray, 34
Chaucer, Geoffrey, 69
Clairmont, Claire, 46, 52, 67, 83, 87, 129, 132-3, 139, 159, 160, 213
Clairmont-Byron, Clara Allegra, 67, 70, 76, 83, 87, 93, 96, 97, 129, 133,143, 146, 147, 159, 160
Clare, John, 179
Clark, James, 123, 130
Clarke, William, 189
Cobbett, William, 98
Cochran, Peter, 82, 130, 244
Cochrane, Eddie, 46
Colburn, Henry, 190
Coleridge, Samuel Taylor, 82
Colvin, Sydney, 203

Cooper, Alice, 23
Cornwall, Barry, 55
Costello, Elvis, 22
Coulson, Walter, 70
Coward, Noel, iii, 31
Cowden Clarke, Charles, 53
Cox, Kyoko Chan, 74
Cox, Tony, 74
Croker, John Wilson, 27
Cronin, Richard, 26
Crook, Nora, 162, 249, 253
Curtis, Richard, 223
Da Vinci, Leonardo, 217
Dante, 110, 218
Daudet, Alphonse, 22
Dgidi, George Ewane, 109
Dickens, Charles, 17
Dickstein, Morris, 205
Douglass, Frederick, 198
Dowden, Edward, 196
Dryden. John, 65
Dylan, Bob, 31, 214
East India Company, 193
Eastlake, Charles, 193
Edinburgh Review, 124
Eliot, T.S., 205
    'The Waste Land', 208, 210
Epstein, Brian, 31, 45, 112, 149, 158, 168
Euripides, 17
Fawcett, Miillicent, 200
Feldmann-Barrett, Christine, 29
Filicaja, Vincenzo, 82, 213
Foot, Paul, 199, 205
Formby, George, 216
Gallagher, Paul, 242
Gamba, Count Pietro, 162, 175

140; first meeting with Leigh
Hunt, 53; first meeting with
Shelley, 56; influenced by Byron,
26; inner confidence, 90;
inspiration, 21; last meetings with
Shelley, 70; last operation, 58;
last words on Byron, 127;
Negative Capability, 71, 116;
Odes, 100, 104; on 'Don Juan',
114, 126, 127; on poetry, iv, 221;
on Wordsworth, 10; onset of
tuberculosis, 86, 120; plays, 118
quotes Byron's 'Fare Thee Well',
118; reads 'Ode to Pan' to
Wordsworth, 10; responds to
criticism of 'Endymion', 90;
responds to Shelley's invitation,
123; response to Byron's fame,
103; visit to Oxford, 68; walking
tour of Scotland, 85; writes will,
125; last days in Rome, 130; last
known letter, 130; death in
Rome, 133

Works

'Endymion', 66, 69, 70-1, 75-6,
80-1, 87-8, 90-1, 106, 123, 128,
135, Shelley's response to, 107;
'Great Spirits Now on Earth Are
Sojourning', 61; 'Hymn to
Apollo', 66; 'Hyperion', 21, 91,
100, 122, 127, 134, 141, 142,
150, 161, 164, 231; 'La Belle
Dame Sans Merci, 121, 193; 'On
First Looking into Chapman's
Homer', 53; 'Sleep and Poetry',
62, 65; 'Sonnet to Haydon',
89; 'The Eve of St Agnes', 100,
104;'To Autumn', 22, 63, 93,
113-4, 122, 200; 'To Solitude',
4, 44, 45, 53; 'When I have
fears', 76; 'Written in Disgust of
Vulgar Superstition', 64;
'Written on the Day that Mr
Leigh Hunt left prison', 37, 89;
'La Belle Dame Sans Merci',
104, 121; 'The Fall of Hyperion',
110; 'Keen, fitful gusts', 55;
'Lamia', 100, 110, 165; 'Poems
Published in 1820', 121-2, 164,
167

Keats, Tom, 76, 79, 98
Kennedy, James, 175
Kent, Elizabeth, 165
Kenyon Jones, Christine, 198
Kesey, Ken, 152
King, Martin Luther, 109
Kinnaird, Douglas, 172
Klein, Allen, 153, 168, prunes
expenditure at Apple Corps, 170
Kuersten, Erich, 105
Lamb, Lady Caroline, 25
Landor, Walter Savage, 144
Langley Moore, Doris, 176, 177
Lear, Edward, 194
Leavis, F.R., 205

Leigh Hunt, James, 39, 68, 141

and 'Skimpole', 17; and 'The
'Mask of Anarchy', 117; arrives
in Italy, 161; attacked in

Discover the Romantics through song!
at
<u>www.thefirstfabfour.co.uk</u>

Shelley Songs
*(a 40-minute song cycle with
some of his greatest lyrics)*
Seven Byronic Songs
(themed on Byron's final journey to Greece)
John Keats's Sublime Single
(two great Keats poems in song)

plus, video lives of the poets:

The Still Unfolding Life of Percy Bysshe Shelley
Byron and Greece – a poet's fight for Freedom
with narration by Benjamin Zephaniah
The Strangely Encouraging Life of John Keats
narrated by John Webster.

and at
<u>www.johnmwebster.co.uk</u>

***The Rime of the Asian Highway: a 70s overland
journey to India remembered in verse***